HOLIDAYS and SPECIAL OCCASIONS CHARTED DESIGNS

Over 225 Motifs for Counted Cross-Stitch and Other Needlecrafts

Georgia L. Gorham
and
Jeanne M. Warth

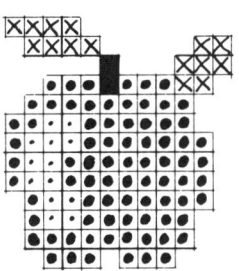

DOVER PUBLICATIONS, INC.
NEW YORK

Copyright © 1981 by Dover Publications, Inc.
All rights reserved under Pan American and International
Copyright Conventions.

Published in Canada by General Publishing Company, Ltd., 30
Lesmill Road, Don Mills, Toronto, Ontario.
Published in the United Kingdom by Constable and Company,
Ltd., 10 Orange Street, London WC2H 7EG.

Holidays and Special Occasions Charted Designs was origi-
nally published by Dover Publications, Inc., in 1981 under the
title *Charted Designs for Holidays and Special Occasions.*

International Standard Book Number: 0-486-24192-0
Library of Congress Catalog Card Number: 81-66838

Manufactured in the United States of America
Dover Publications, Inc.
31 East 2nd Street
Mineola, N.Y. 11501

Introduction

This collection consists of over 225 motifs charted for use in different forms of needlework such as needlepoint, latch-hooking, counted cross-stitch, crochet and knitting. The motifs include those designs most wanted by needleworkers for special occasions: holidays such as Easter and Christmas, special days such as birthdays, graduation and back-to-school, borders to complement the designs, and lettering in three styles that say it all. The book is arranged with similar motifs grouped together; i.e., all of the Valentines appear on pages 2–3, Independence Day on pages 29–31, and Halloween on pages 33–35.

All of the designs are plotted on easy-to-read grids of ten squares to the inch. Bear in mind that the finished piece of needlework will not be the same size as the charted design unless you happen to be working on fabric that has the same number of threads per inch as the chart has squares per inch. To determine how large a finished design will be, divide the number of stitches in the design by the thread-count of the fabric. For example, if a design that is 112 stitches wide by 140 stitches deep is worked on a 14-count cloth, divide 112 stitches by 14 to get 8 and 140 by 14 to get 10; so the worked design will measure 8″ × 10″. The same design worked on 22-count fabric would measure approximately 5″ × 6½″.

Use a single small motif on needlepoint canvas to make a coaster, pincushion, pocket or small picture. Repeat the same design or put several different ones together to make a pillow, a belt or a wall hanging. Latch hook or quick point one design onto heavy-weight rug canvas and you will have a pillow. Combine several to make a rug.

The designs can be worked directly onto needlepoint canvas by counting off the correct number of warp and woof squares shown on the chart, each square representing one stitch to be taken on the canvas. If you prefer to put some guidelines on the canvas, make certain that your marking medium is waterproof. Use either non-soluble inks, acrylic paints thinned appropriately with water so as not to clog the holes in the canvas, or oil paints mixed with benzine or turpentine. Felt-tipped pens are very handy, but check the labels carefully because not all felt markers are waterproof. It is a good idea to experiment with any writing materials on a piece of scrap canvas to make certain that all material is waterproof. There is nothing worse than having a bit of ink run onto the needlepoint as you are blocking it.

For counted cross-stitch, select an evenweave fabric such as cotton aida or hardanger cloth. Each square on the chart represents one cross-stitch taken over the intersection of the threads of the fabric. When working with an evenweave linen in which there are some thin threads and some nubbier or fatter ones, the cross-stitch is worked over two threads each way. Make certain that all of the stitches cross in the same direction. Gingham or other checkered material can also be used for cross-stitch by making the crosses over the checks from corner to corner. If you wish to embroider a cross-stitch design onto a fabric which does not have an evenweave, baste a lightweight Penelope canvas to the fabric. The design can then be worked from the chart by making crosses over the double mesh of the canvas, being careful not to catch the threads of the canvas in the sewing. When the design is completed, the basting stitches are removed, and the horizontal and then the vertical threads of the canvas are removed, one strand at a time, with a tweezers. The cross-stitch design will remain on the fabric.

Charted designs can be worked in duplicate stitch over the squares formed by stockinette stitch in knitting or afghan stitch in crochet. The patterns can also be knitted directly into the work by working with more than one color, as in Fair Isle knitting. The wool not in use is always stranded across the back of the work. When it has to be stranded over more than five stitches, it should be twisted around the wool in use on every third stitch, thus preventing long strands at the back of the work. When a number of colors are used, a method known as "motif knitting" is employed. In this method short lengths of wool are cut and wound on bobbins, using a separate bobbin for each color and twisting the colors where they meet to avoid gaps in the work, as in knitting argyle socks.

Most of the designs have their own color key. The colors, however, are merely suggestions. You should feel free to substitute your own colors for the ones indicated, thereby creating a design which is uniquely yours. If you decide to create a new color scheme, work it out in detail before beginning a project. To give you a good idea of how the finished project will look, put tracing paper over the design in the book and experiment with your own colors on the tracing paper.

BALLOONS

HOUR GLASS
- ☒ beige
- ⊡ pale gray
- ☐ light brown

PARTY HAT

PARTY BLOWER

COCKTAIL
- ☒ olive green or cherry
- ☐ pale green or pink

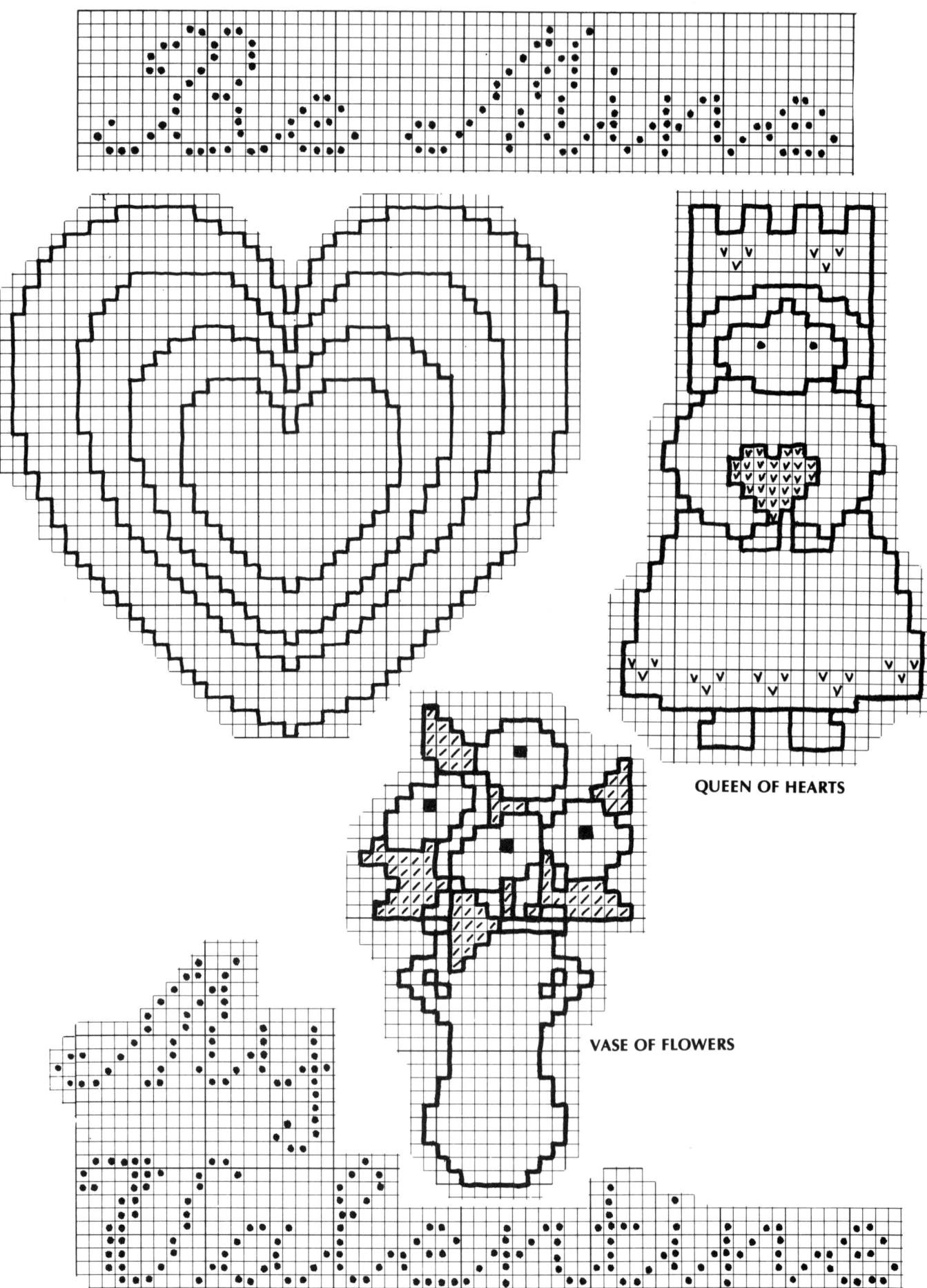

QUEEN OF HEARTS

VASE OF FLOWERS

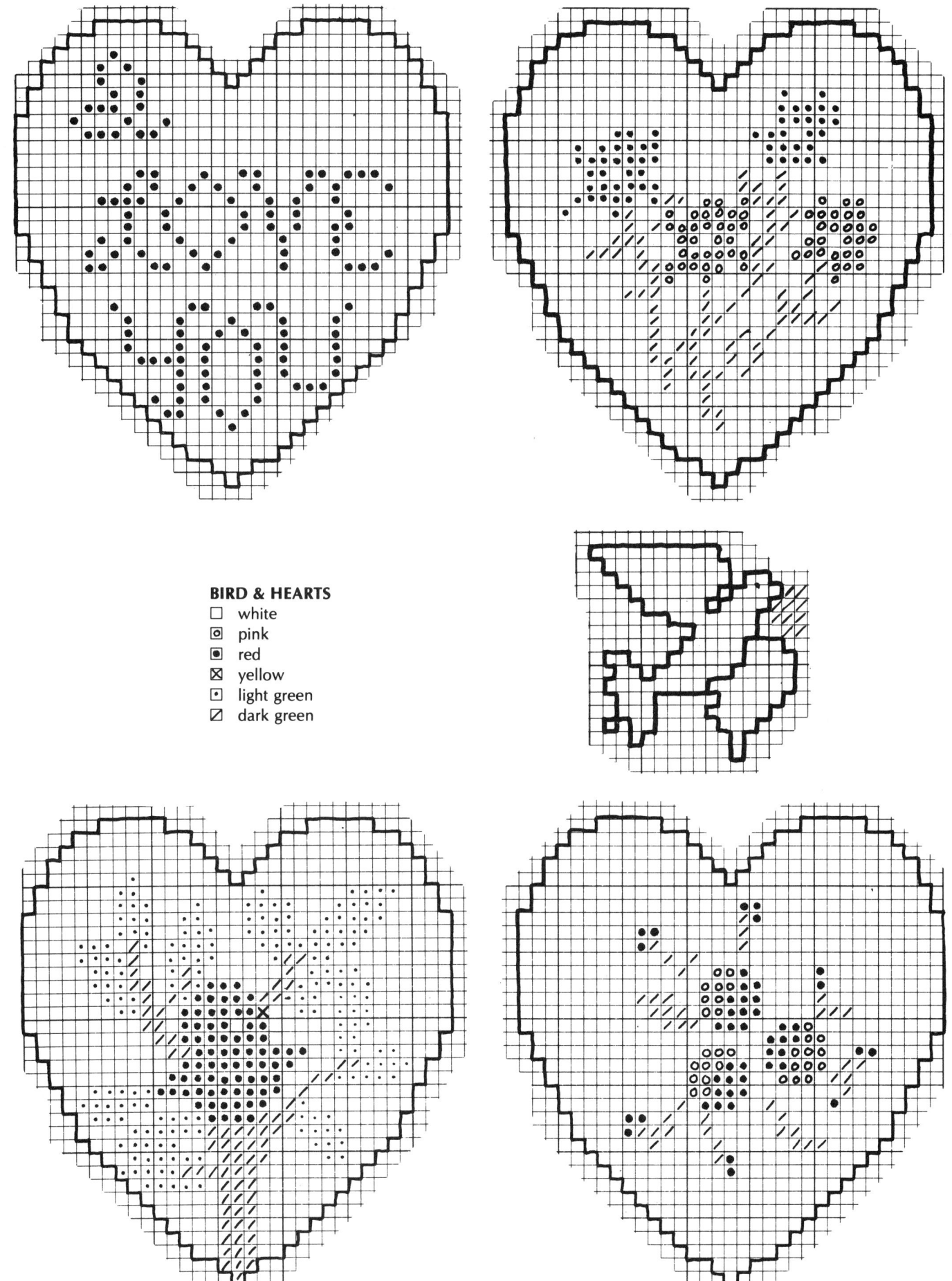

BIRD & HEARTS

☐ white
⊡ pink
▣ red
⊠ yellow
⊡ light green
⊘ dark green

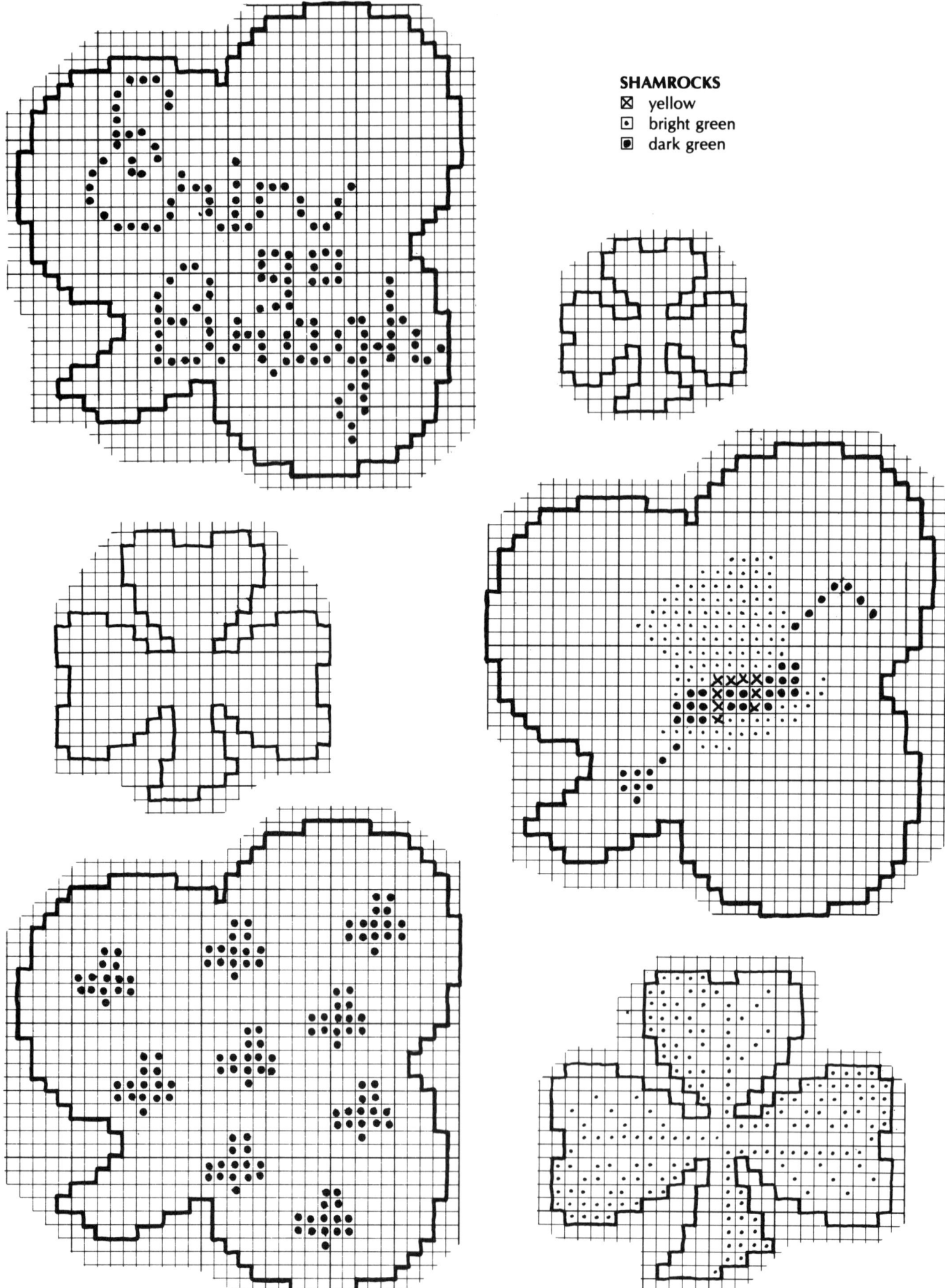

SHAMROCKS
- ⊠ yellow
- ⊡ bright green
- ▣ dark green

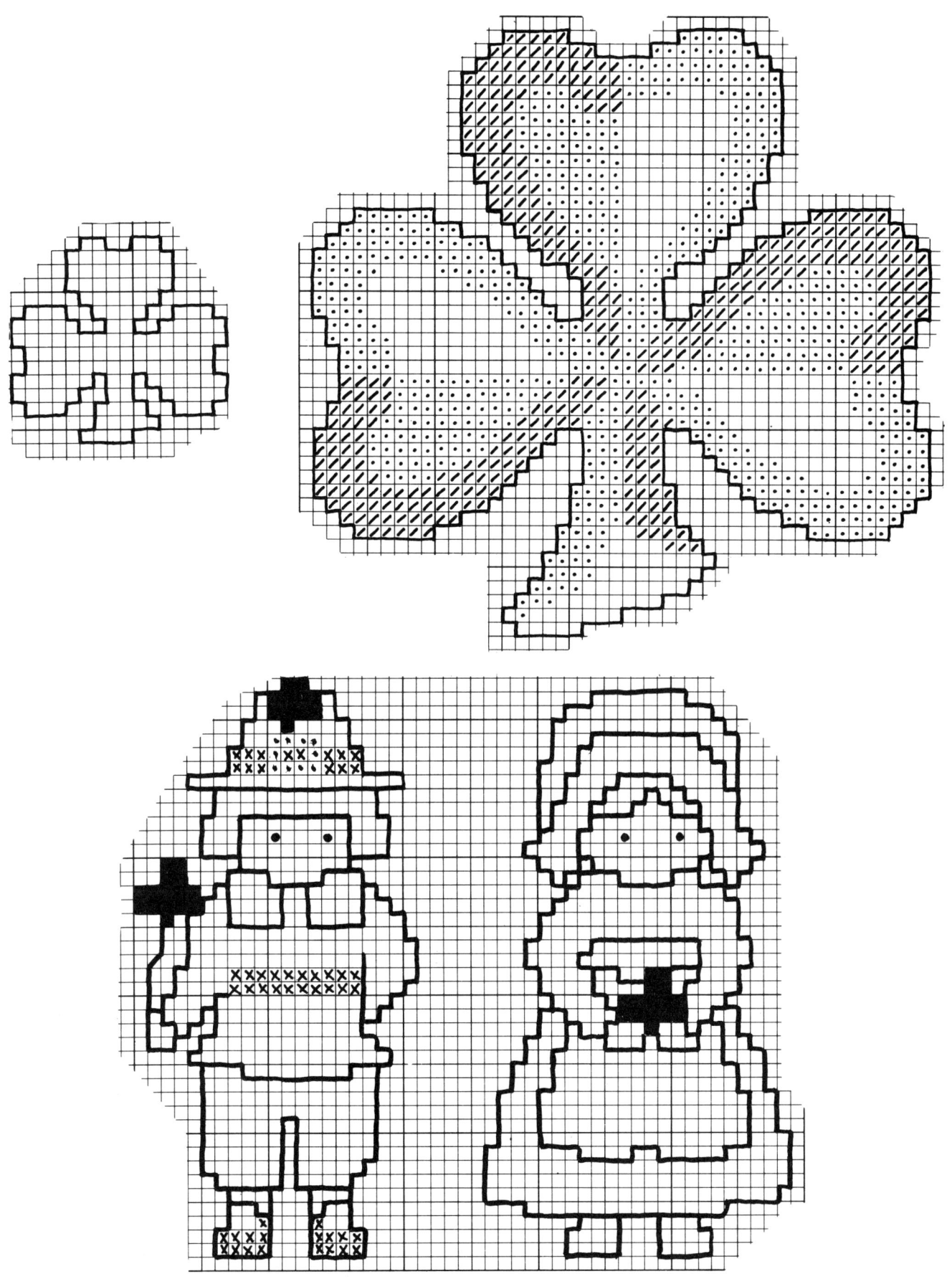

MR. & MRS. IRELAND

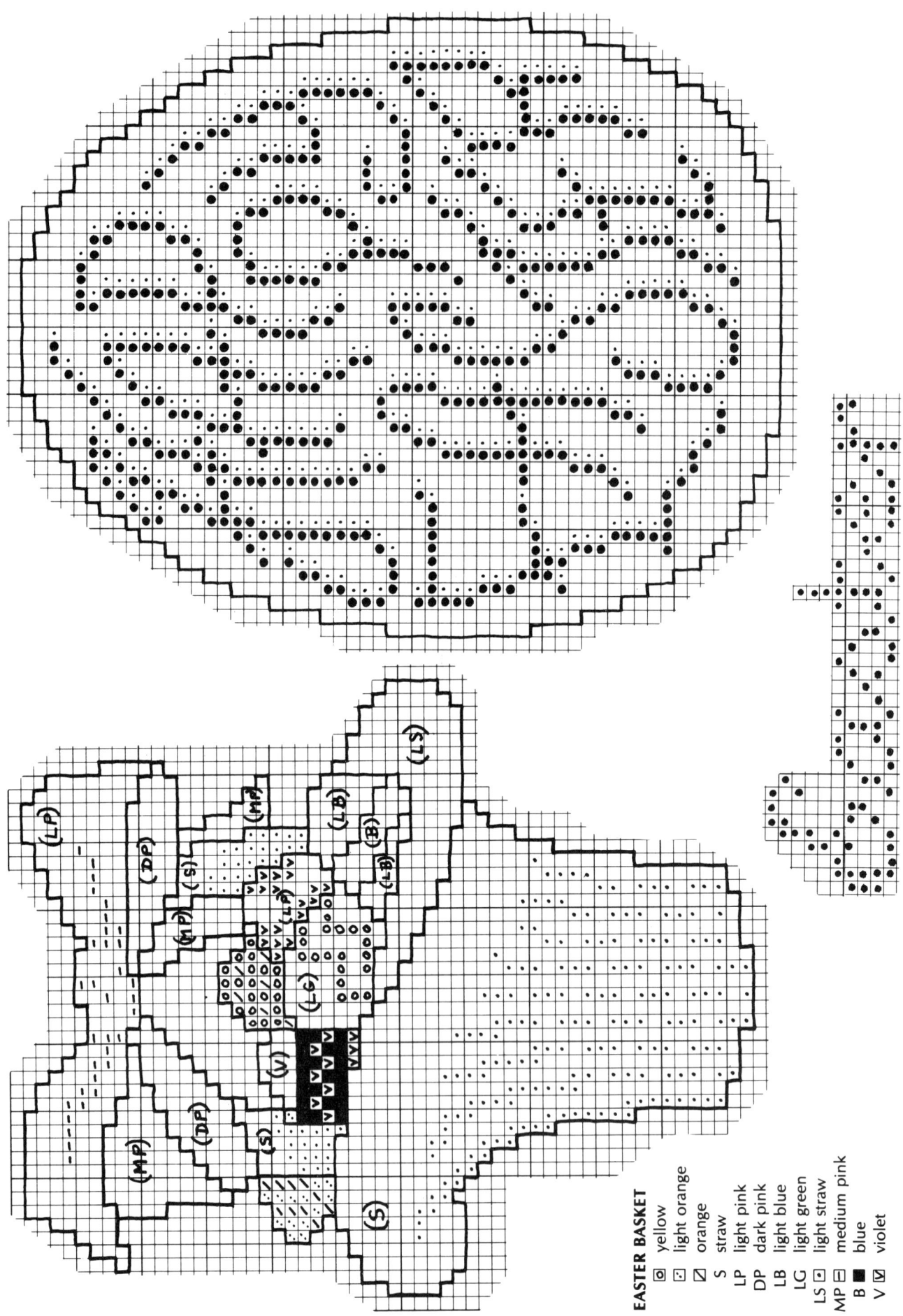

EASTER BASKET
- ⊡ yellow
- ⋮ light orange
- ⧄ orange
- S straw
- LP light pink
- DP dark pink
- LB light blue
- LG light green
- LS light straw
- MP ⊟ medium pink
- B ■ blue
- V ⊻ violet

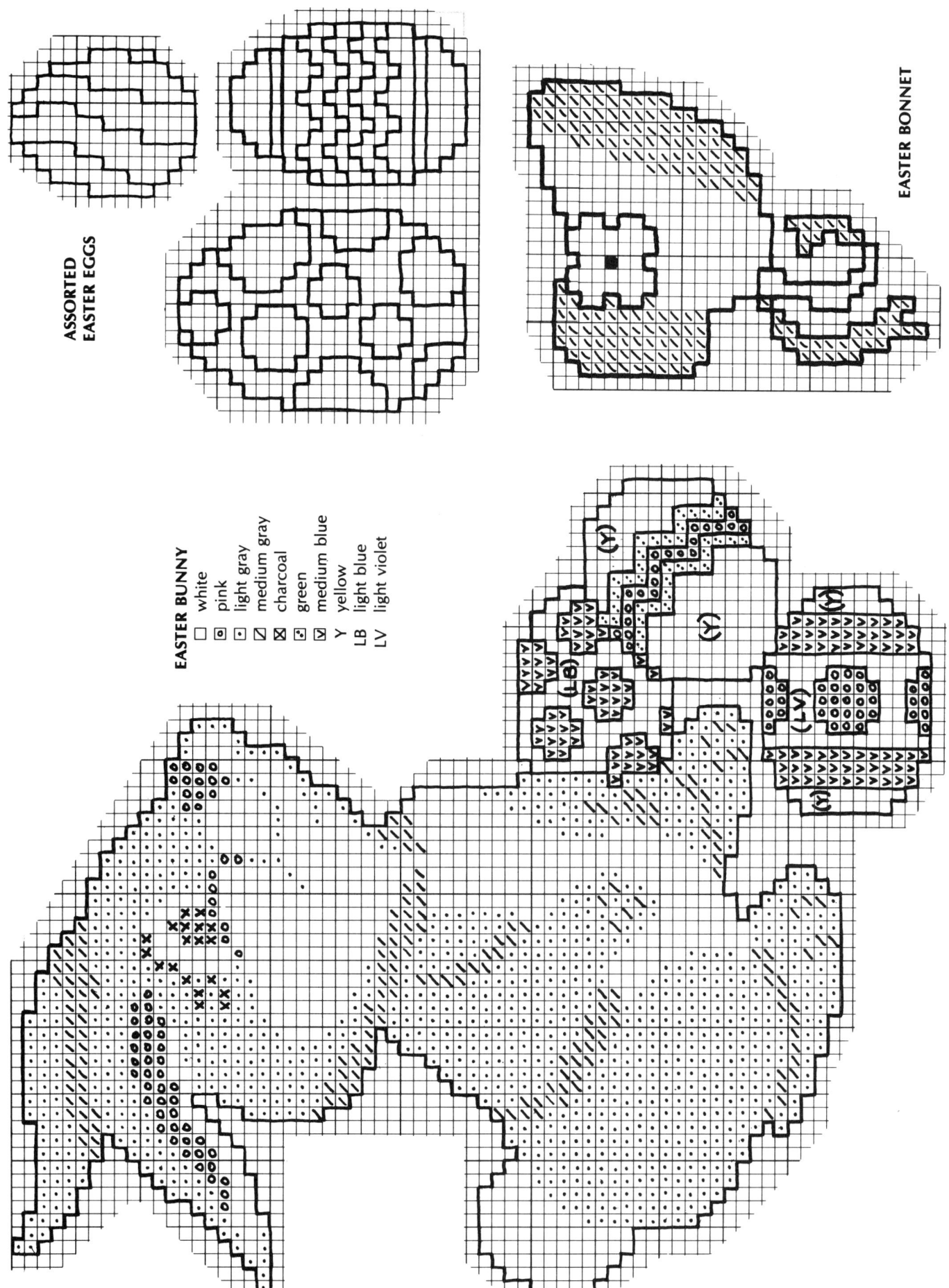

ASSORTED
EASTER EGGS

EASTER BONNET

EASTER BUNNY
- ☐ white
- ⊙ pink
- ⊡ light gray
- ◪ medium gray
- ☒ charcoal
- ▣ green
- ☑ medium blue
- Y yellow
- LB light blue
- LV light violet

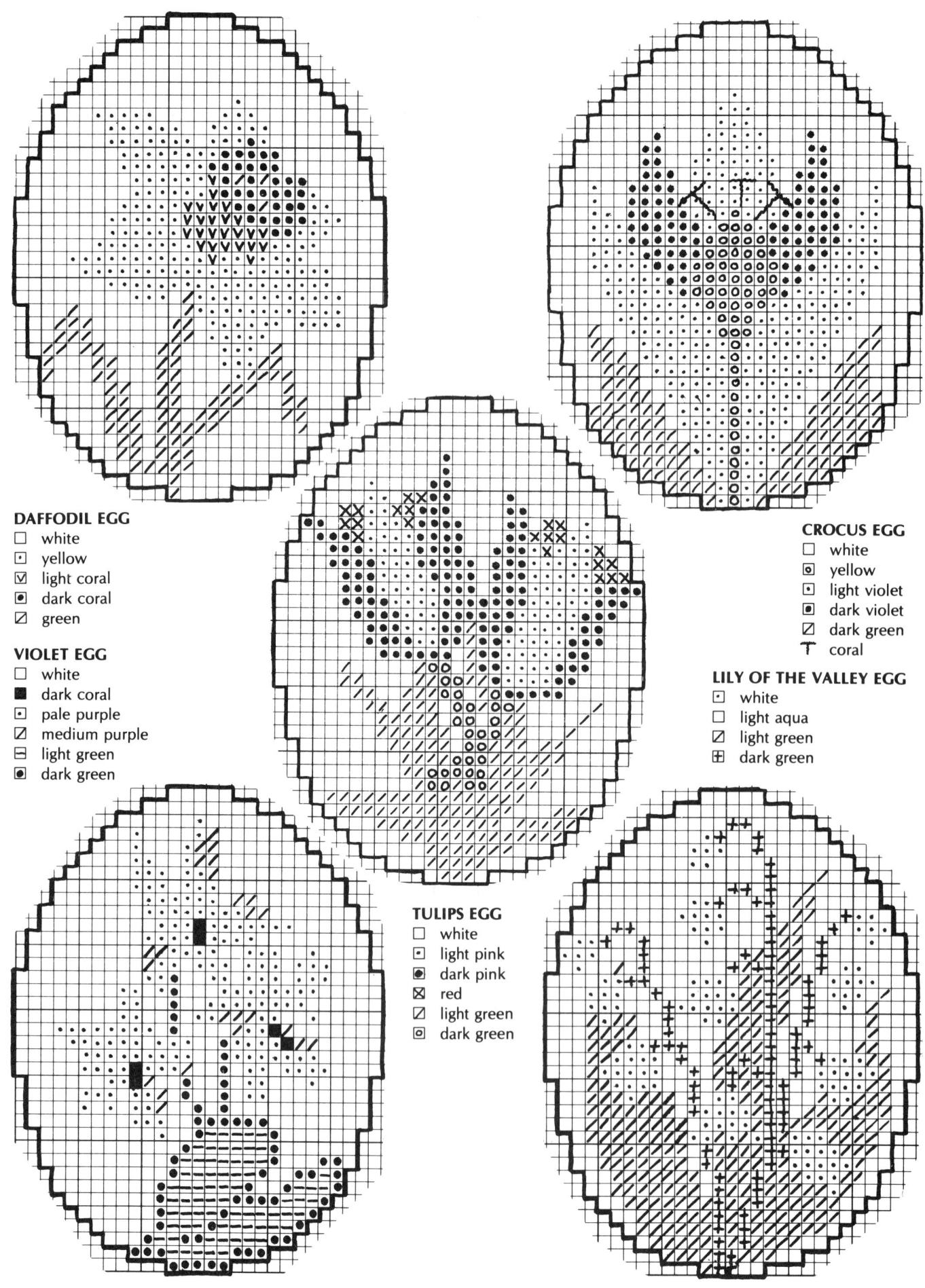

DAFFODIL EGG
- ☐ white
- ⊡ yellow
- ☑ light coral
- ⊙ dark coral
- ☐ green

VIOLET EGG
- ☐ white
- ■ dark coral
- ⊡ pale purple
- ☑ medium purple
- ⊟ light green
- ⊙ dark green

CROCUS EGG
- ☐ white
- ⊙ yellow
- ⊡ light violet
- ⊙ dark violet
- ☑ dark green
- T coral

LILY OF THE VALLEY EGG
- ⊡ white
- ☐ light aqua
- ☑ light green
- ⊞ dark green

TULIPS EGG
- ☐ white
- ⊡ light pink
- ⊙ dark pink
- ☒ red
- ☑ light green
- ⊡ dark green

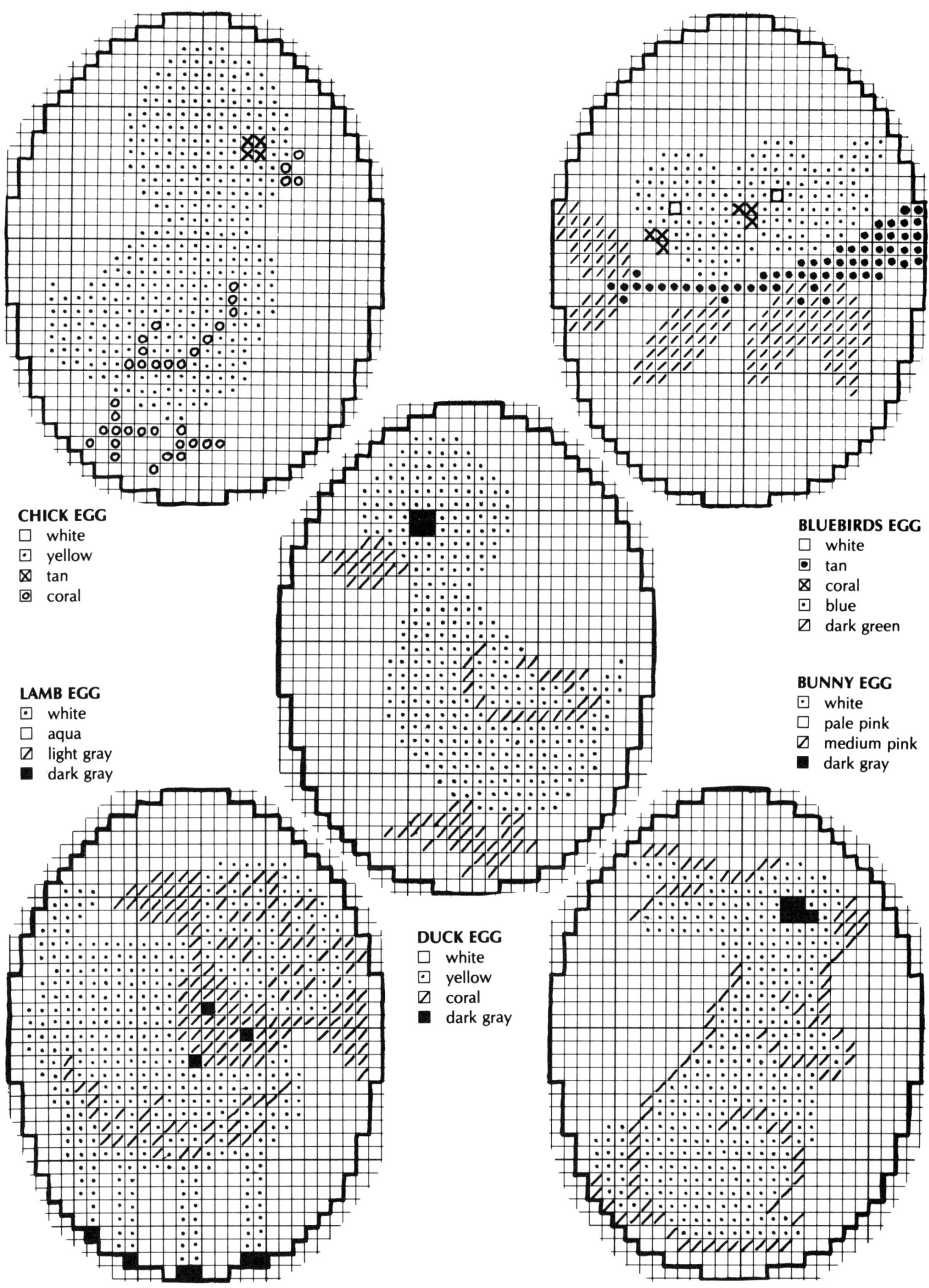

CHICK EGG
☐ white
⊡ yellow
⊠ tan
◉ coral

LAMB EGG
⊡ white
☐ aqua
▨ light gray
■ dark gray

BLUEBIRDS EGG
☐ white
◉ tan
⊠ coral
⊡ blue
▨ dark green

BUNNY EGG
⊡ white
☐ pale pink
▨ medium pink
■ dark gray

DUCK EGG
☐ white
⊡ yellow
▨ coral
■ dark gray

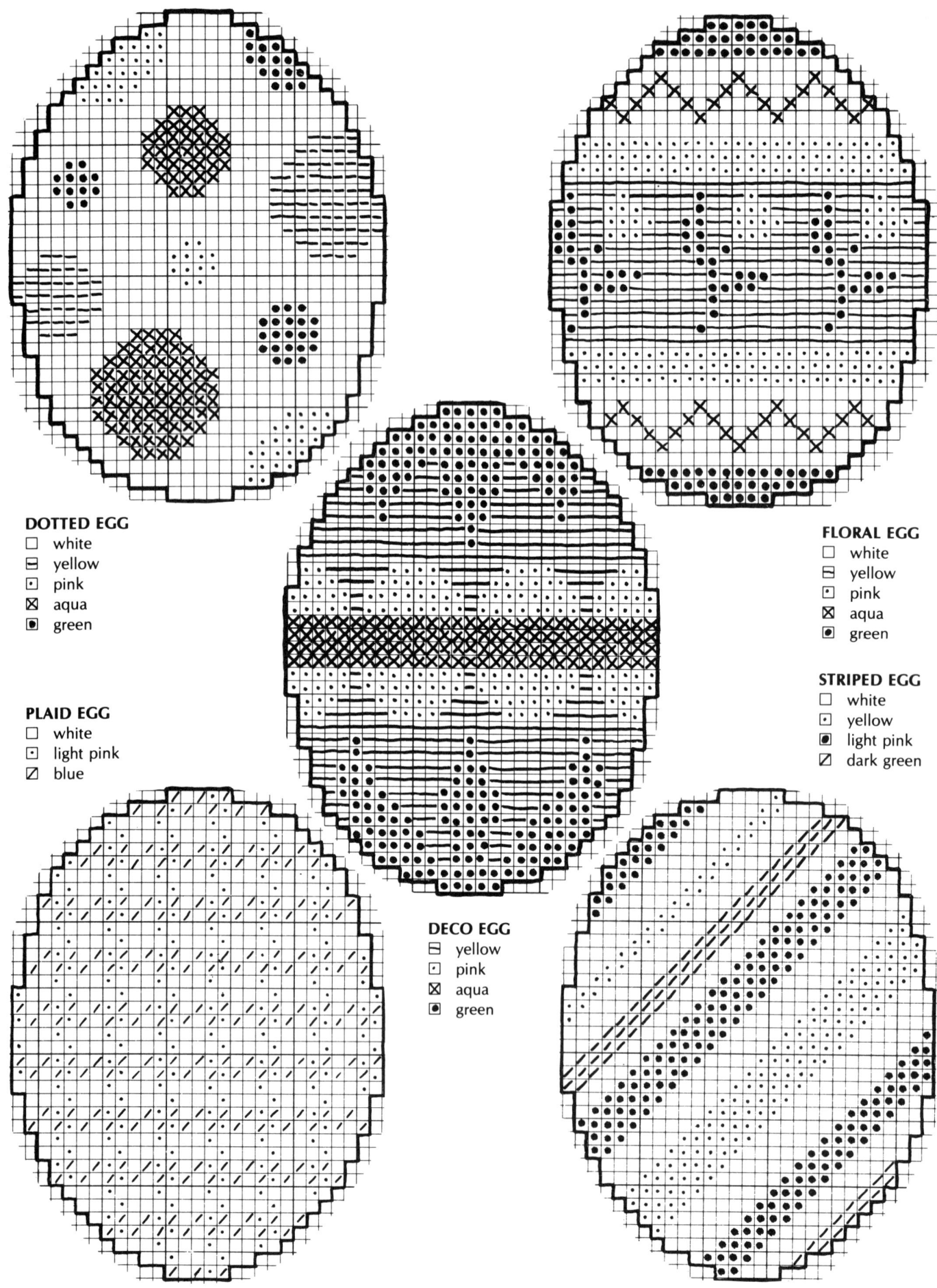

DOTTED EGG
- ☐ white
- ⊟ yellow
- ⊡ pink
- ☒ aqua
- ◉ green

PLAID EGG
- ☐ white
- ⊡ light pink
- ☑ blue

DECO EGG
- ⊟ yellow
- ⊡ pink
- ☒ aqua
- ◉ green

FLORAL EGG
- ☐ white
- ⊟ yellow
- ⊡ pink
- ☒ aqua
- ◉ green

STRIPED EGG
- ☐ white
- ⊡ yellow
- ◉ light pink
- ☑ dark green

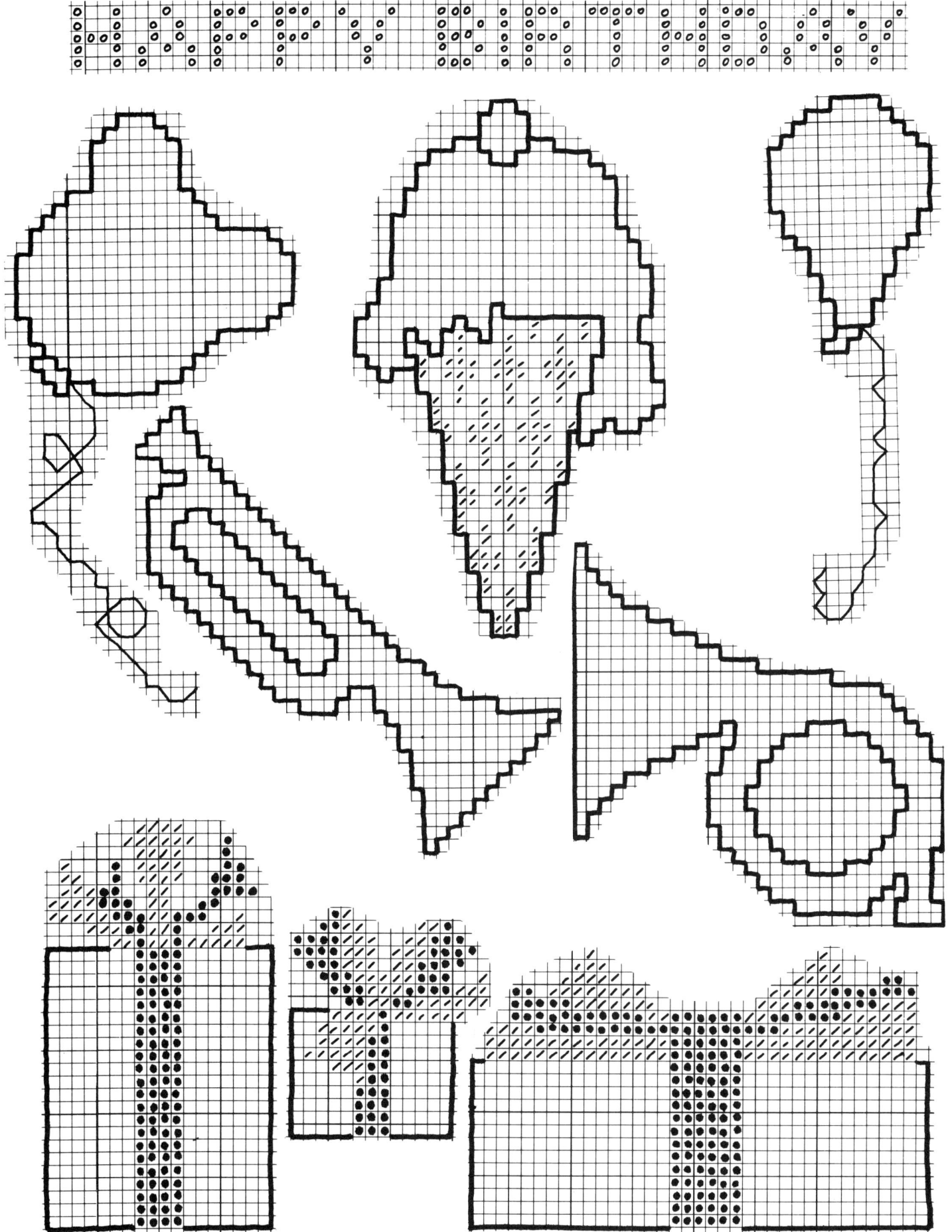

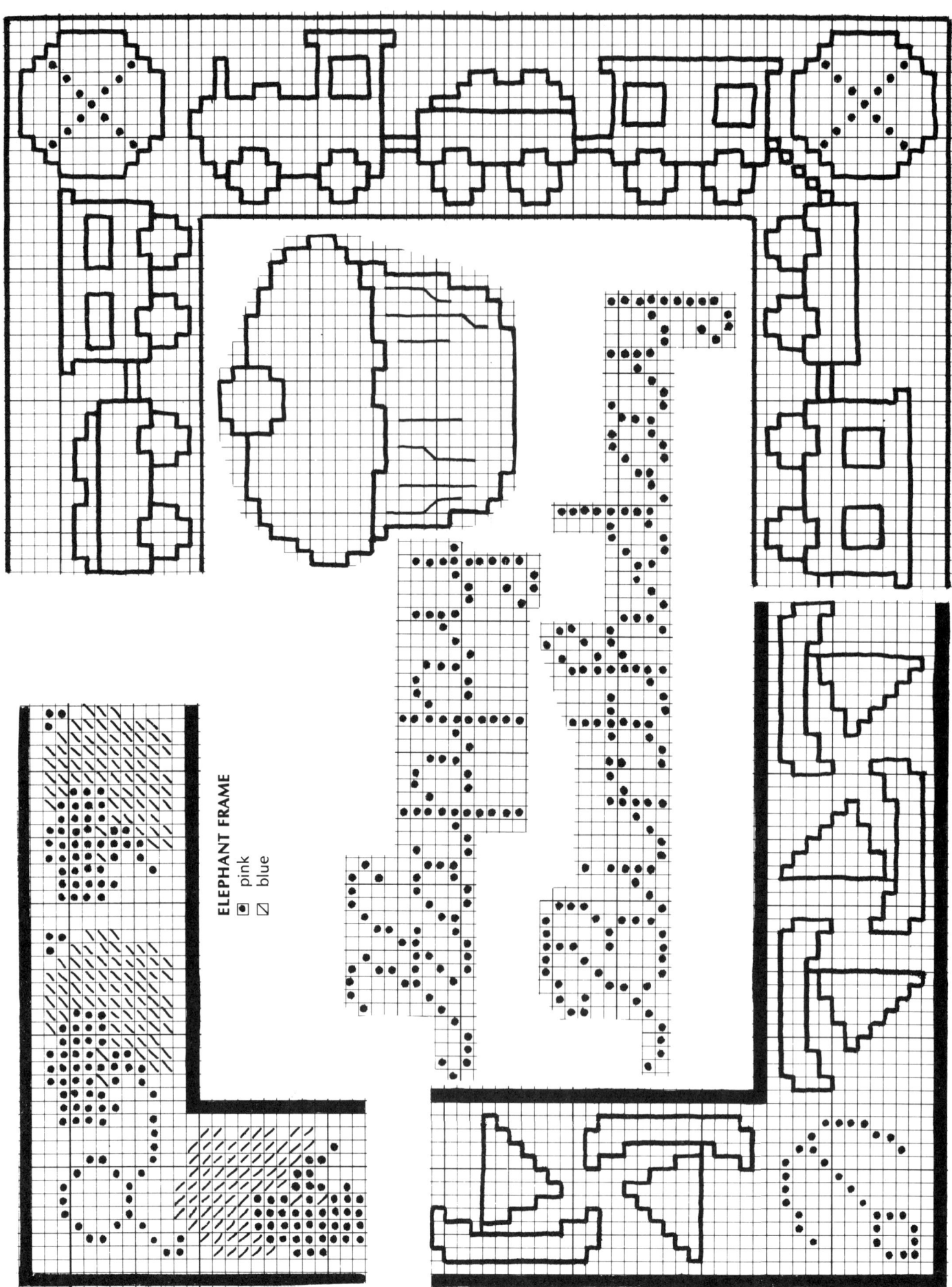

ELEPHANT FRAME

● pink
⧄ blue

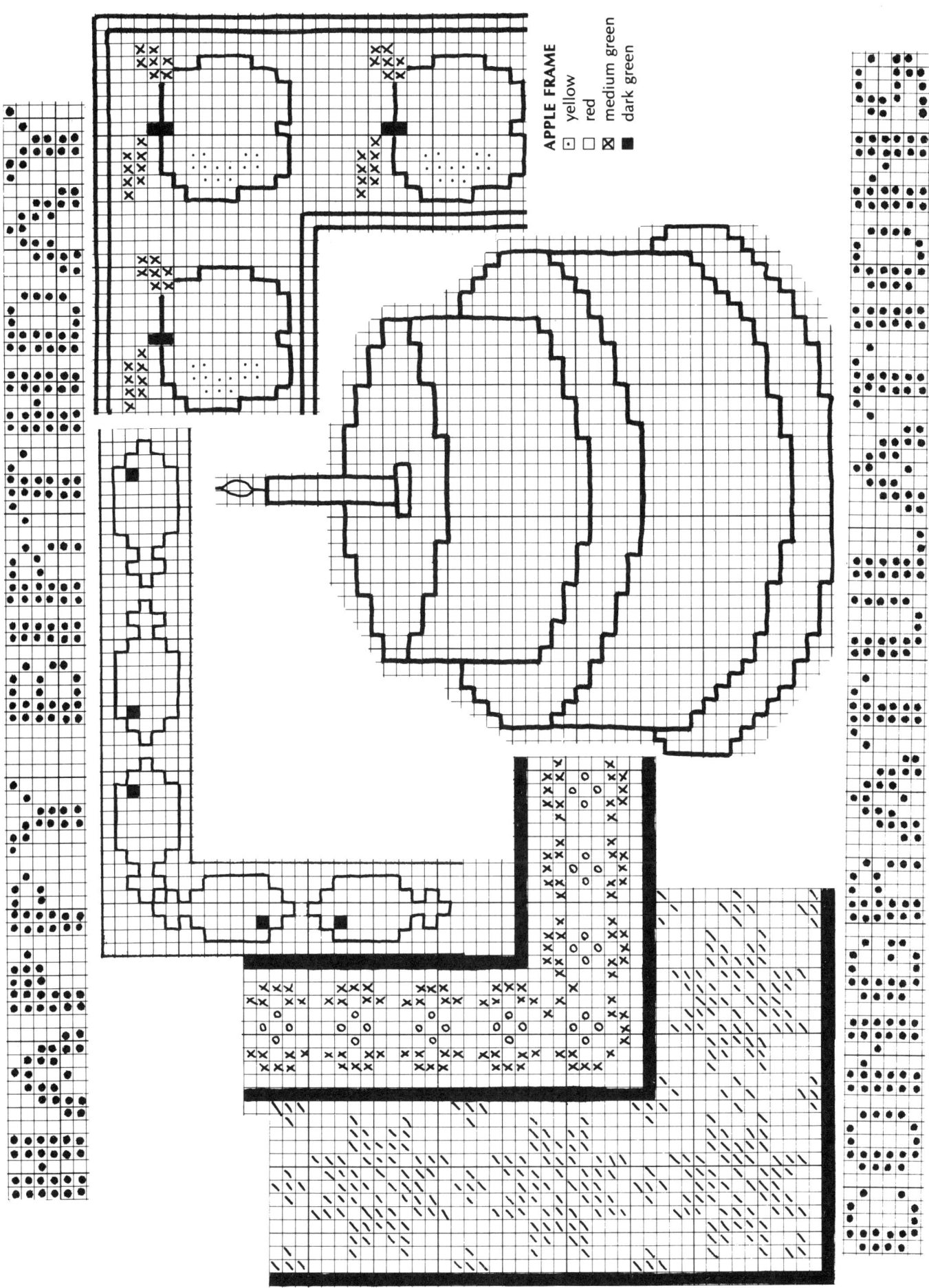

APPLE FRAME
- ⊡ yellow
- ☐ red
- ☒ medium green
- ■ dark green

CLOWN

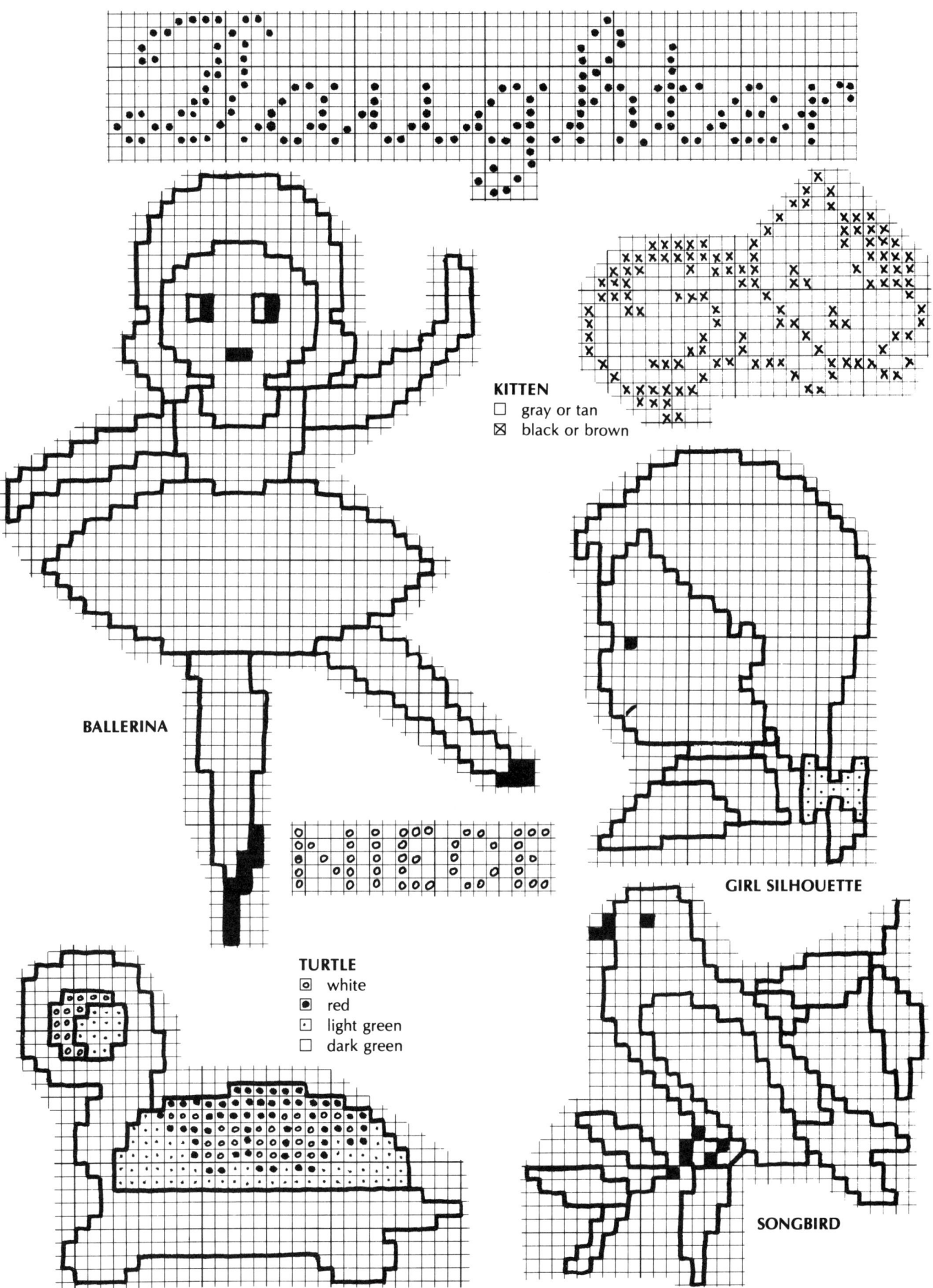

KITTEN
☐ gray or tan
☒ black or brown

BALLERINA

GIRL SILHOUETTE

TURTLE
◉ white
◐ red
⊡ light green
☐ dark green

SONGBIRD

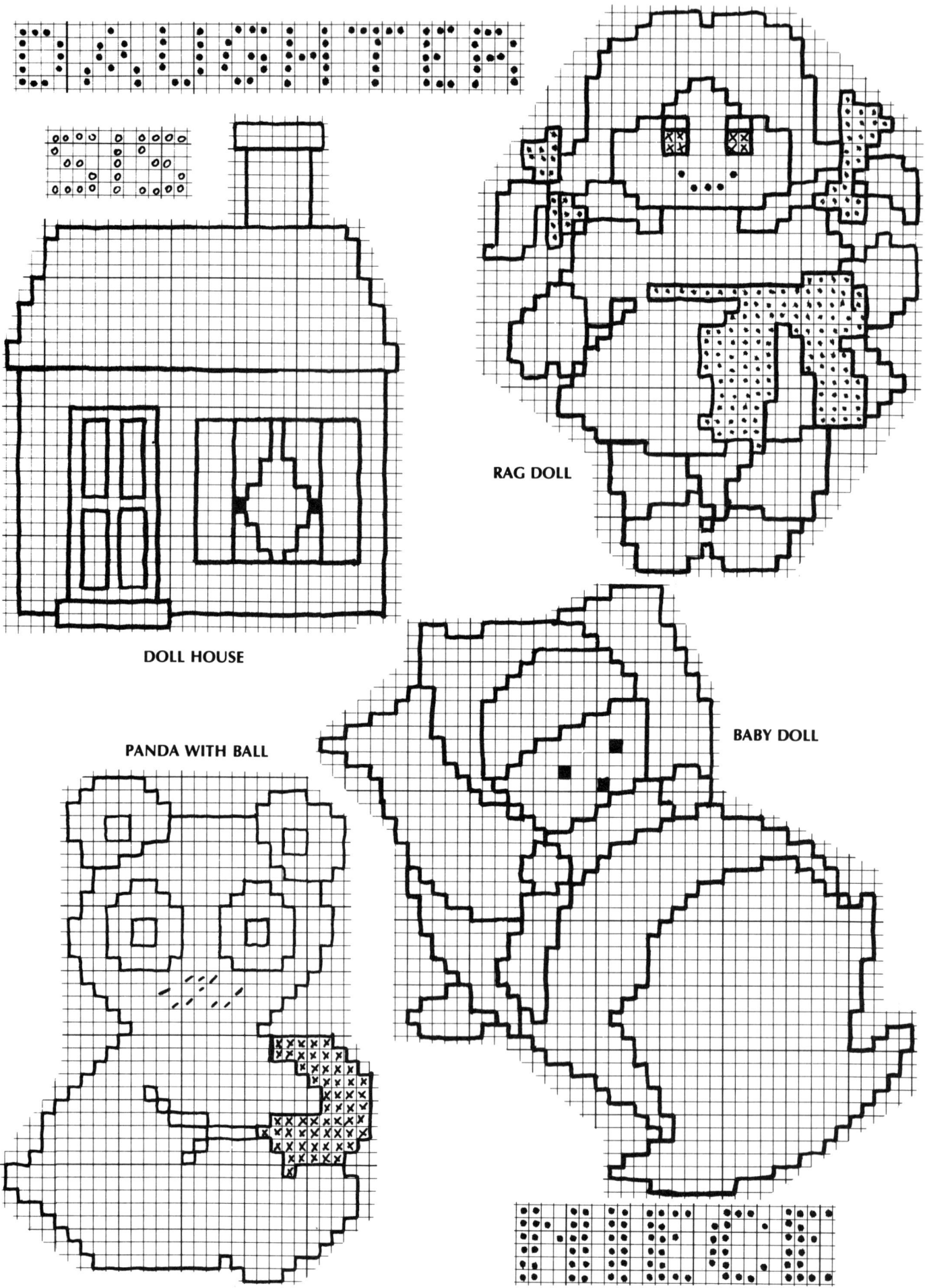

RAG DOLL

DOLL HOUSE

PANDA WITH BALL

BABY DOLL

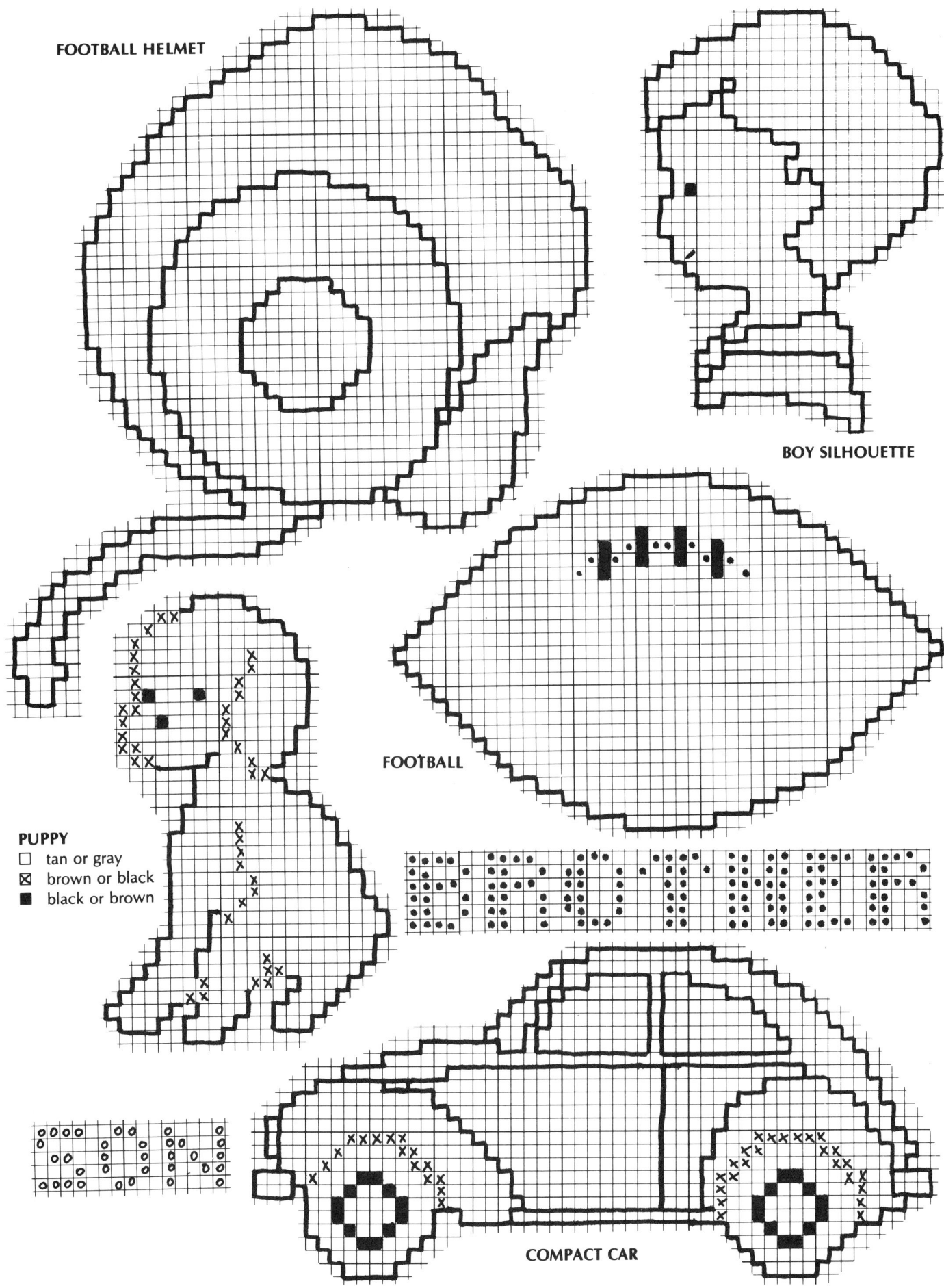

FOOTBALL HELMET

BOY SILHOUETTE

FOOTBALL

PUPPY
- ☐ tan or gray
- ☒ brown or black
- ■ black or brown

COMPACT CAR

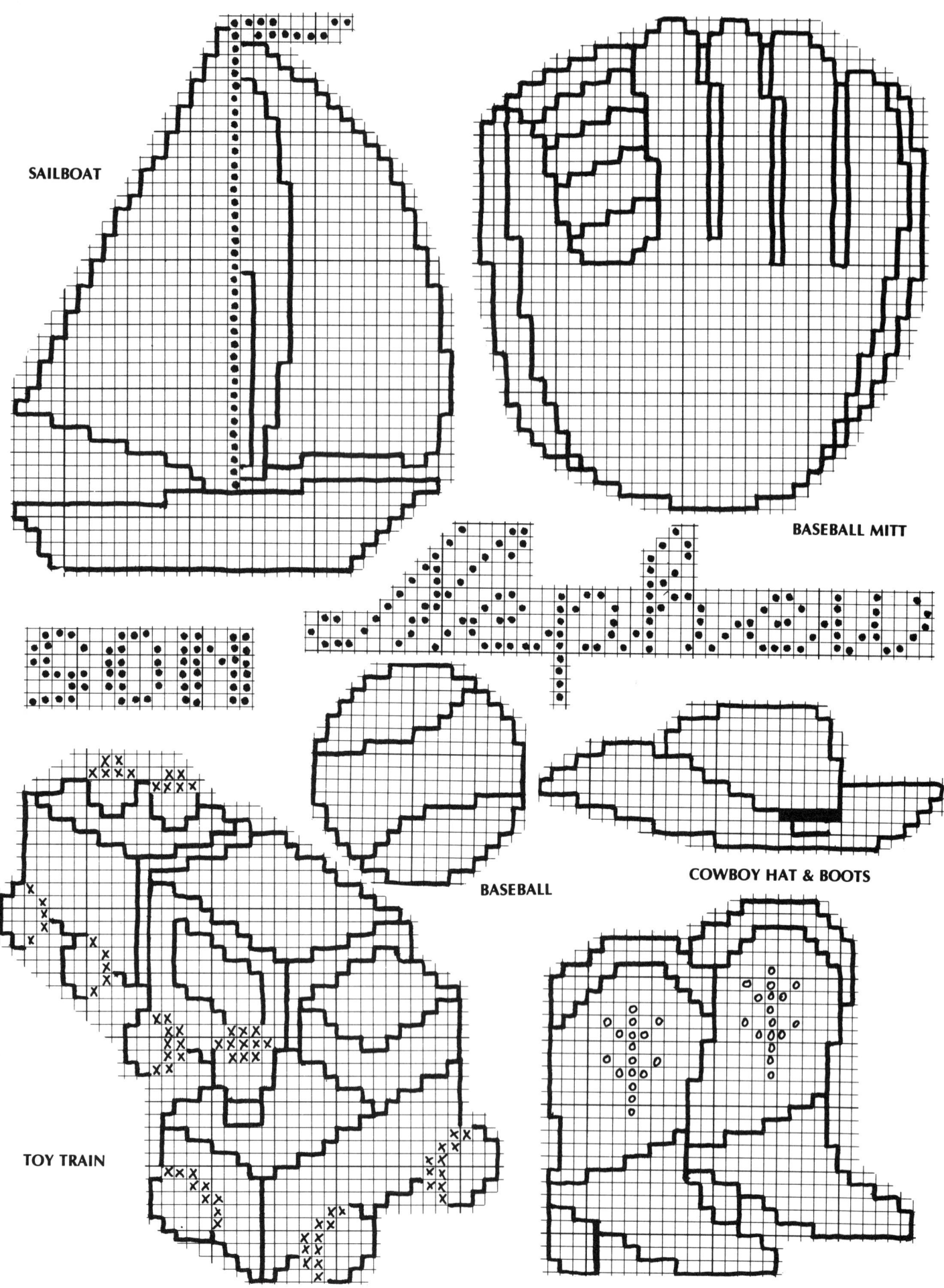

SAILBOAT

BASEBALL MITT

BASEBALL

COWBOY HAT & BOOTS

TOY TRAIN

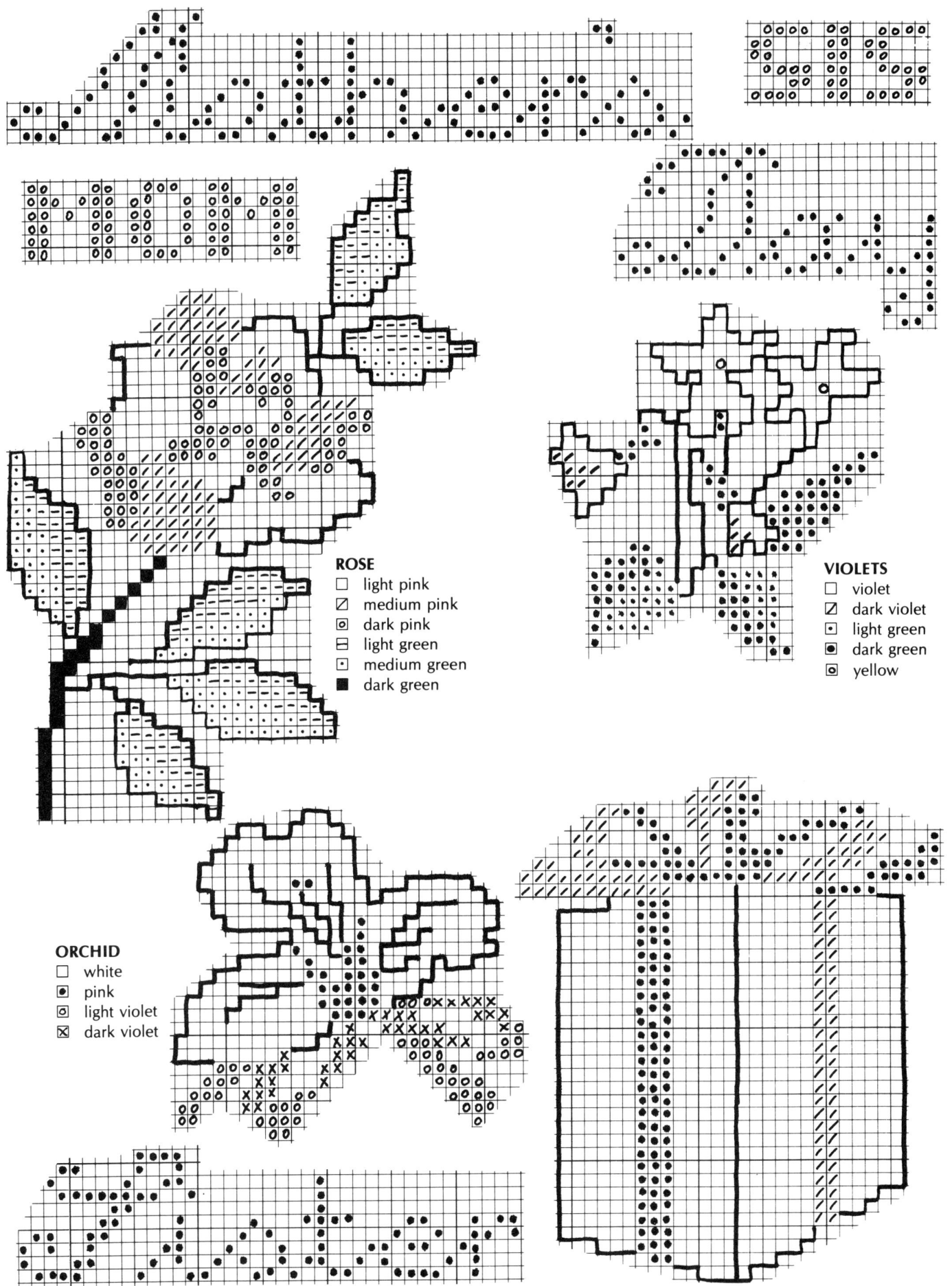

ROSE
- ☐ light pink
- ◨ medium pink
- ⊡ dark pink
- ⊟ light green
- ⊡ medium green
- ◼ dark green

VIOLETS
- ☐ violet
- ◨ dark violet
- ⊡ light green
- ⊙ dark green
- ⊡ yellow

ORCHID
- ☐ white
- ⊙ pink
- ⊡ light violet
- ⊠ dark violet

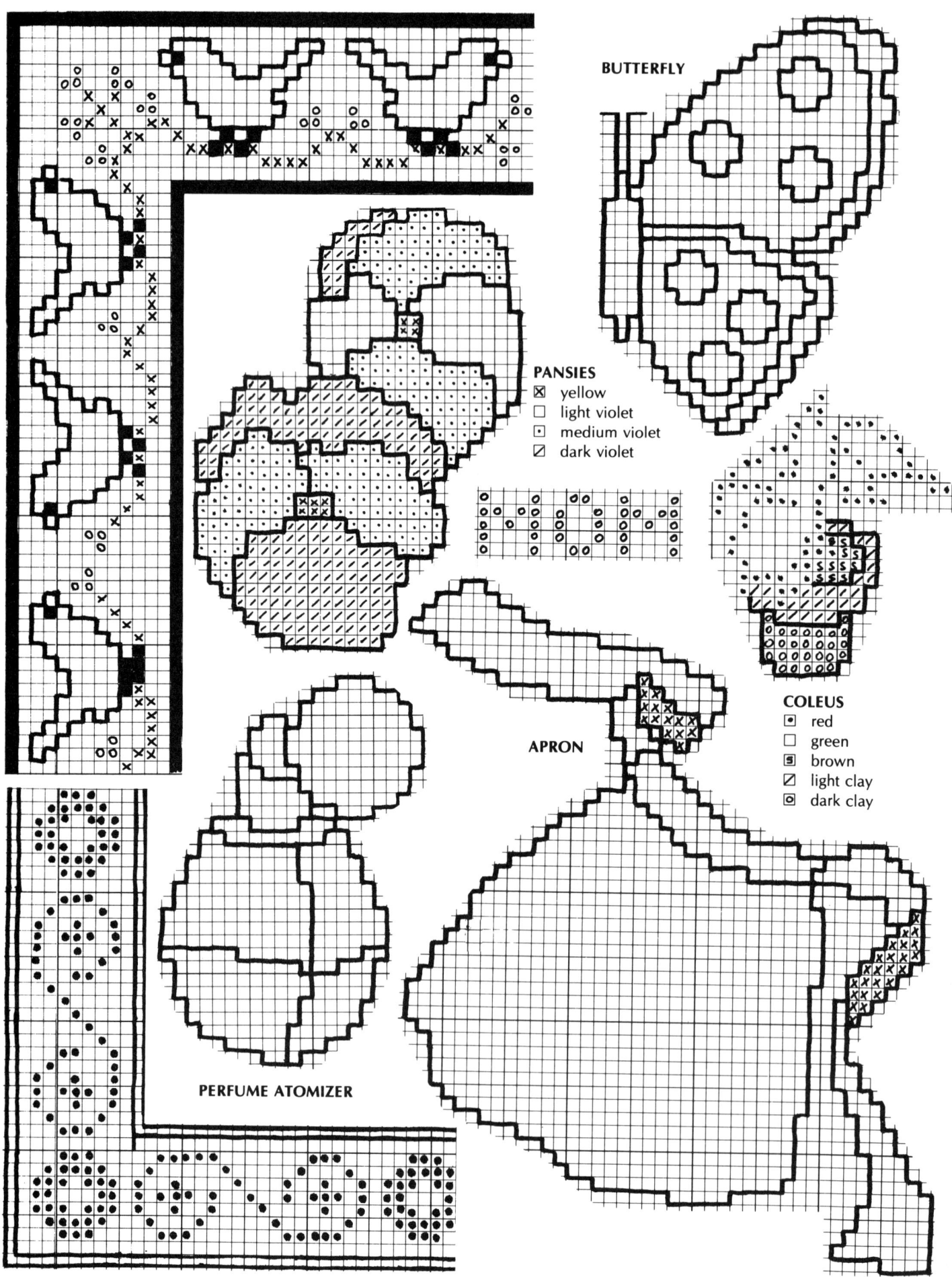

BUTTERFLY

PANSIES
- ⊠ yellow
- ☐ light violet
- ⊡ medium violet
- ⊘ dark violet

COLEUS
- ⊡ red
- ☐ green
- ⑤ brown
- ⊘ light clay
- ⊙ dark clay

APRON

PERFUME ATOMIZER

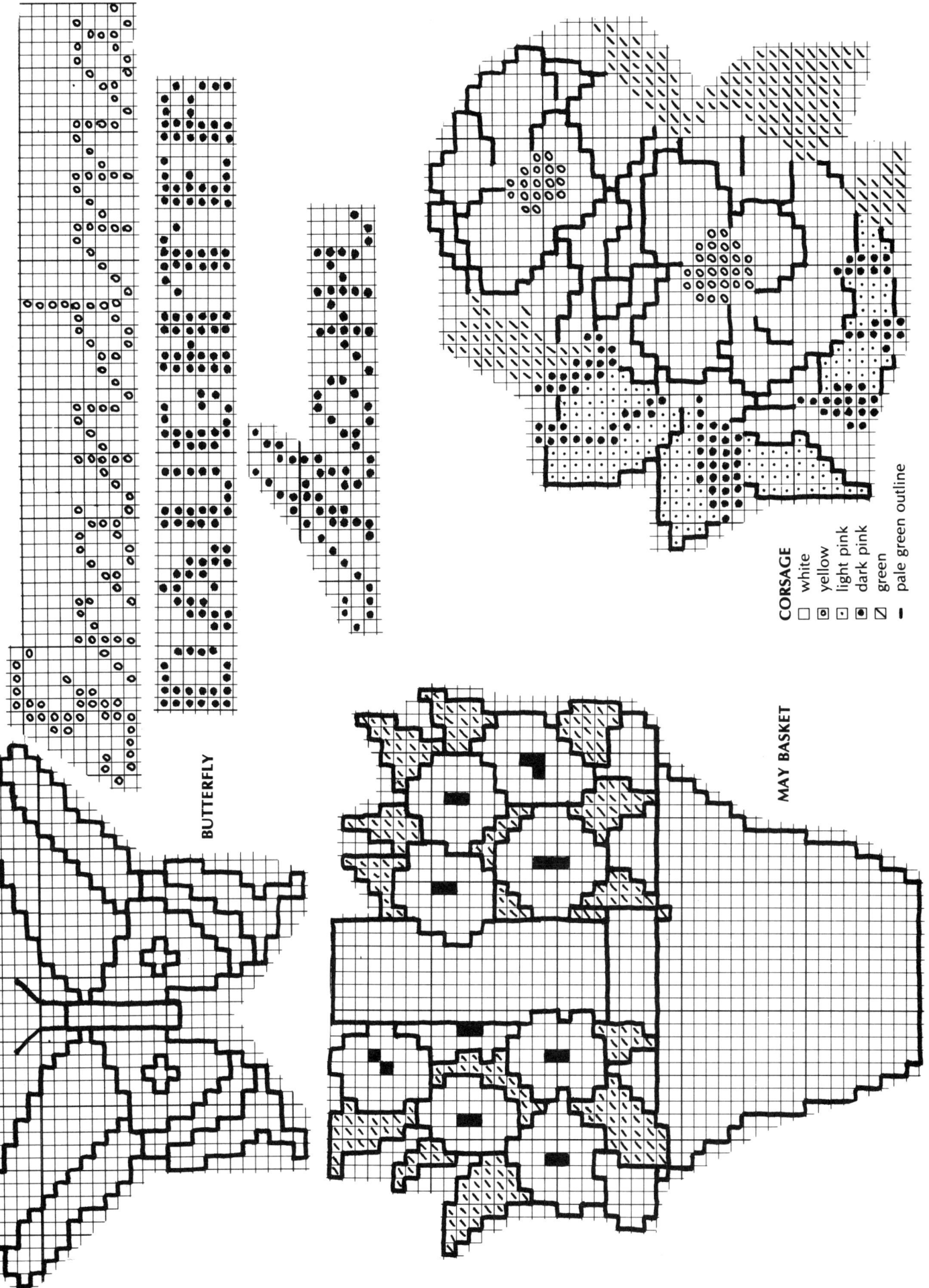

CORSAGE

□ white
◉ yellow
· light pink
● dark pink
⟋ green
▬ pale green outline

BUTTERFLY

MAY BASKET

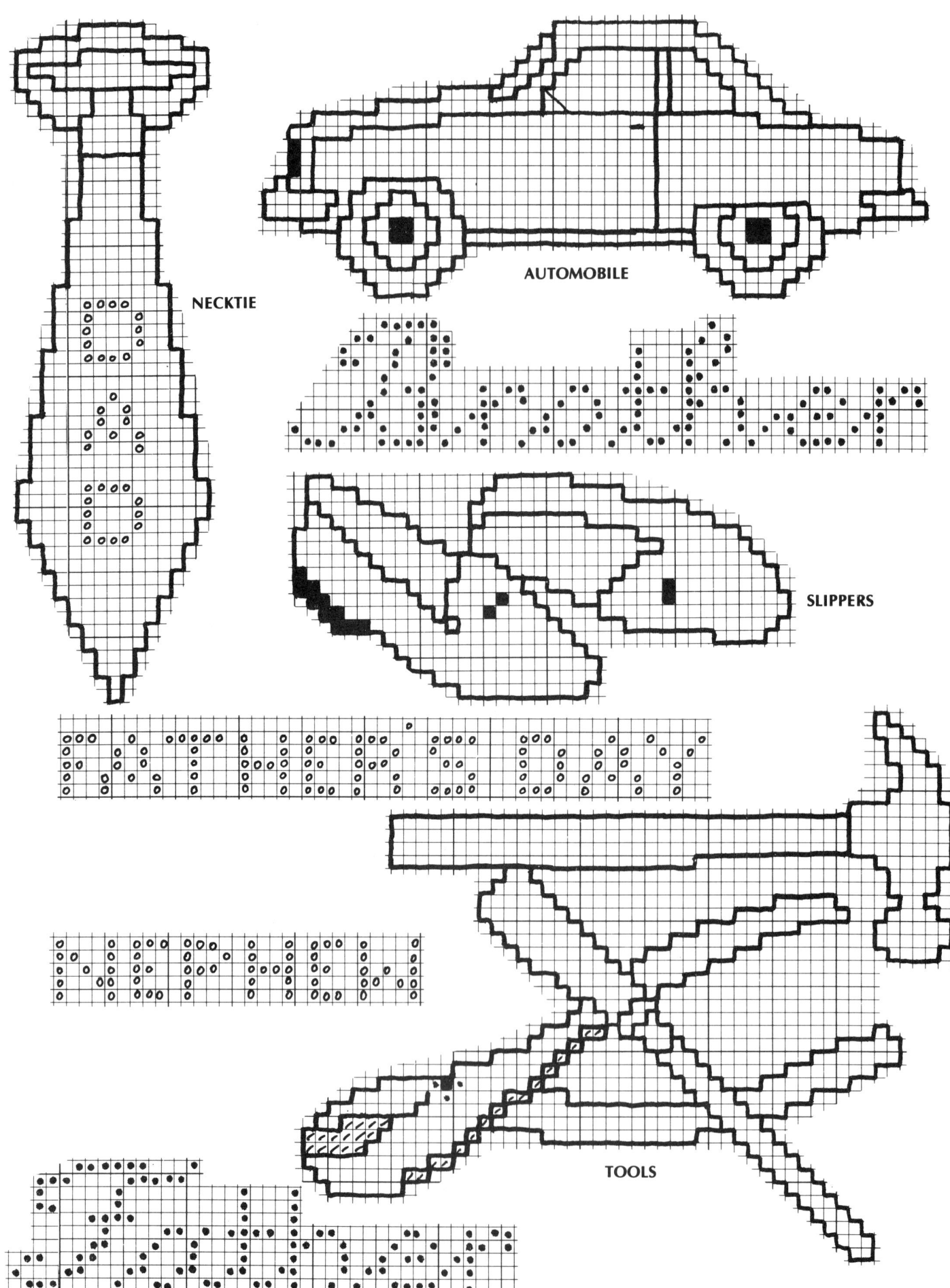

NECKTIE

AUTOMOBILE

SLIPPERS

TOOLS

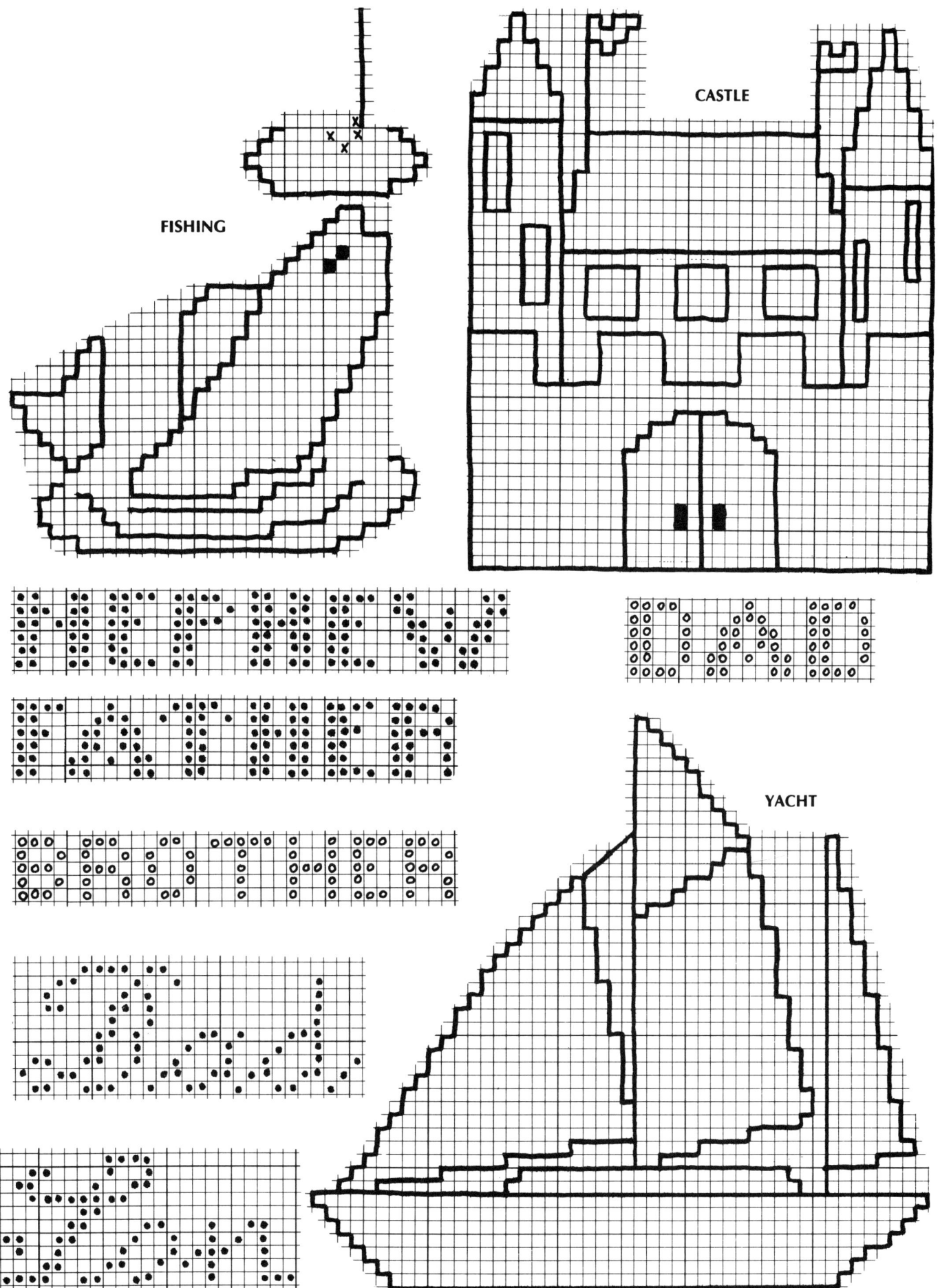

FISHING

CASTLE

YACHT

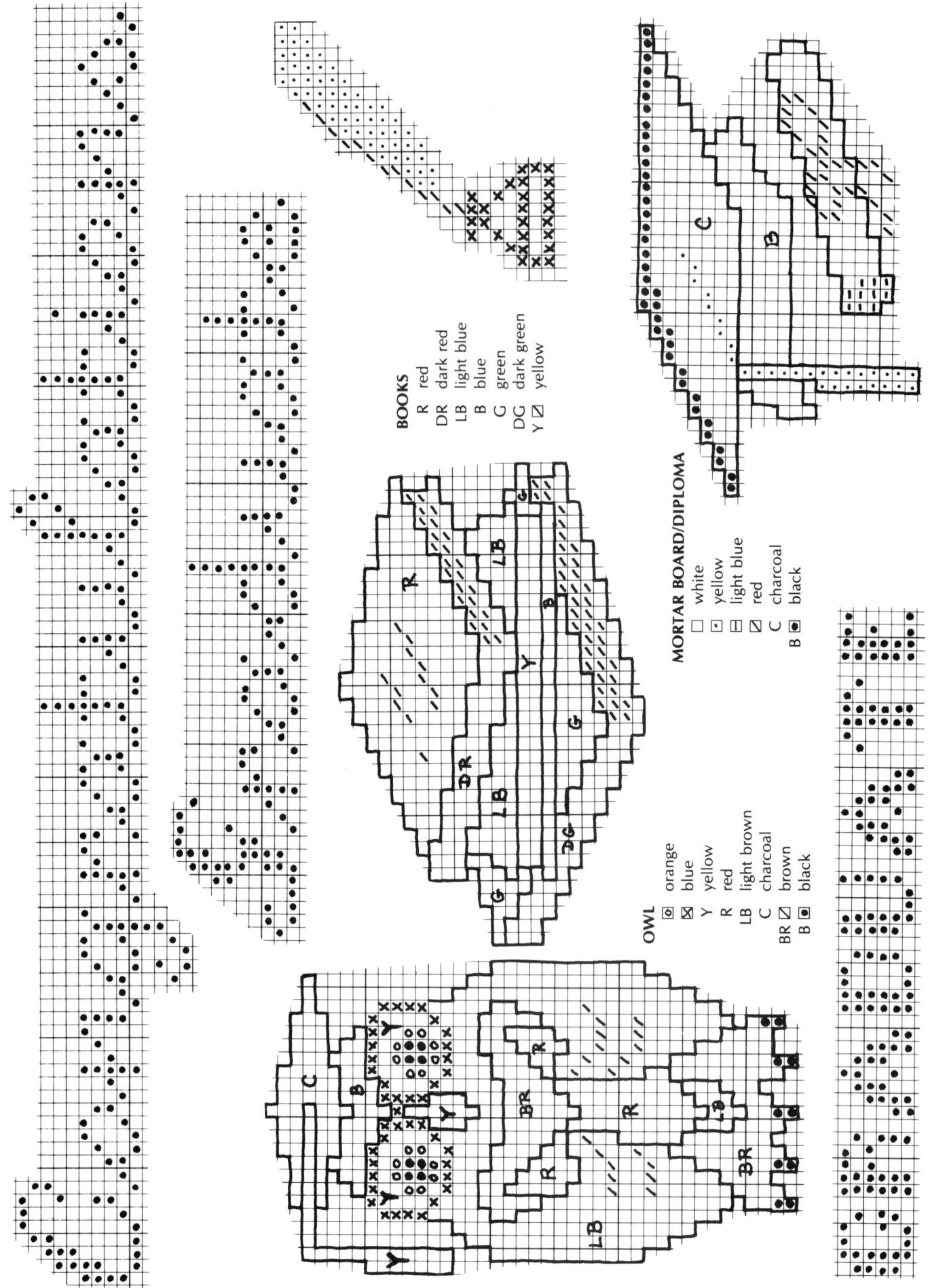

BOOKS

R	red
DR	dark red
LB	light blue
B	blue
G	green
DG	dark green
Y ⊠	yellow

MORTAR BOARD/DIPLOMA

□	white
·	yellow
⊞	light blue
⊘	red
C	charcoal
B ⊡	black

OWL

⊡	orange
⊠	blue
Y	yellow
R	red
LB	light brown
C	charcoal
BR ⊘	brown
B ⊡	black

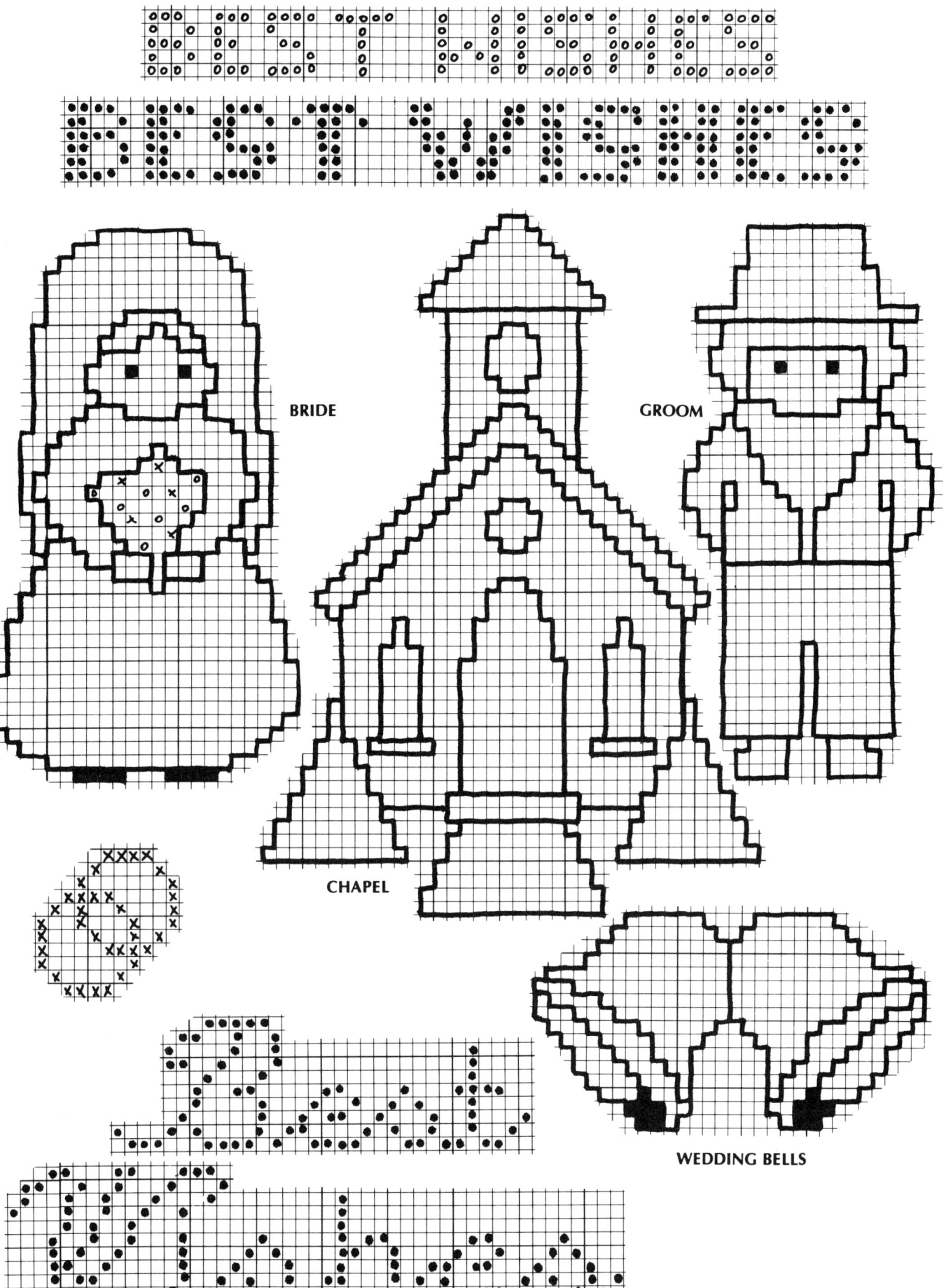

BRIDE

GROOM

CHAPEL

WEDDING BELLS

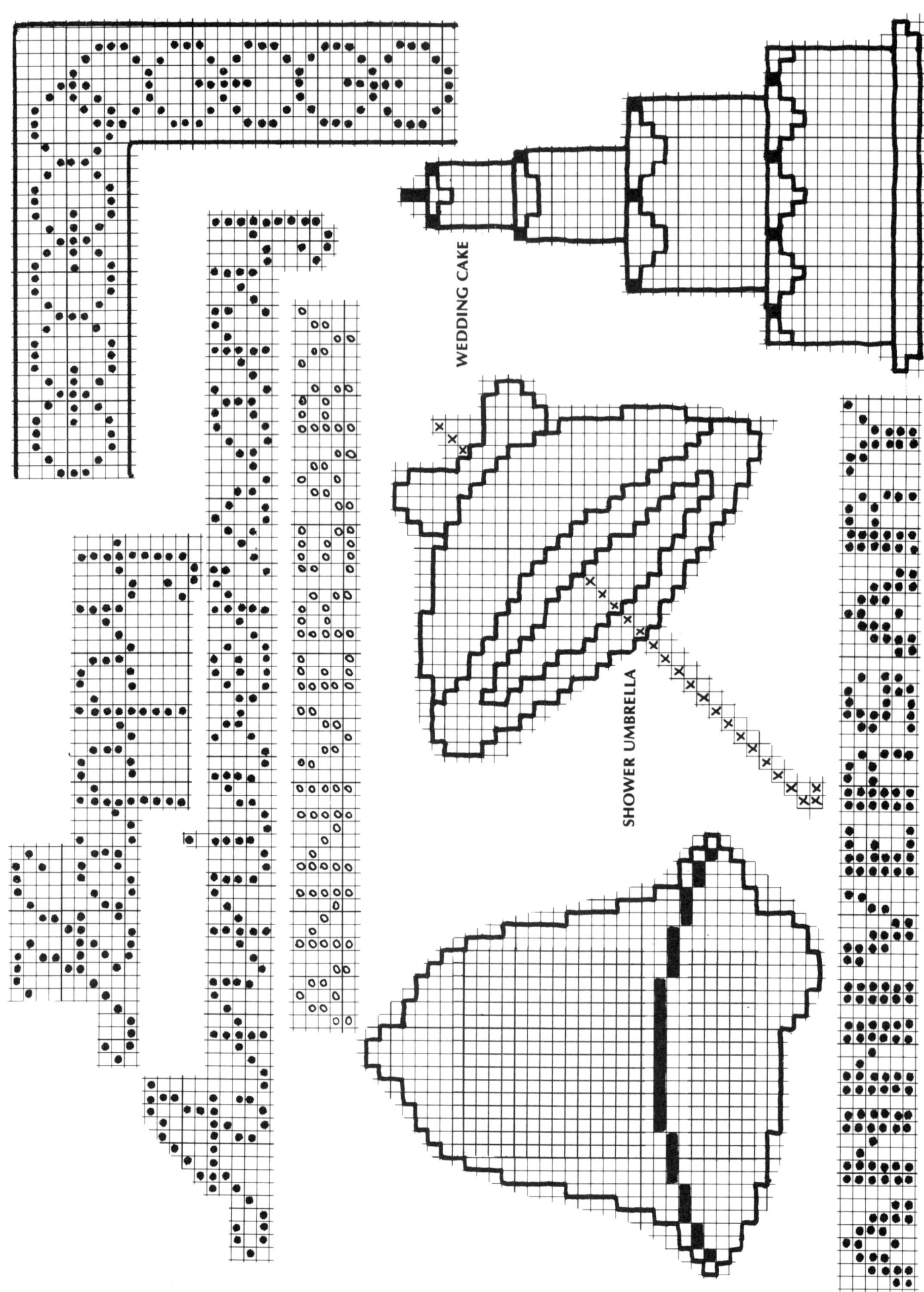

WEDDING CAKE

SHOWER UMBRELLA

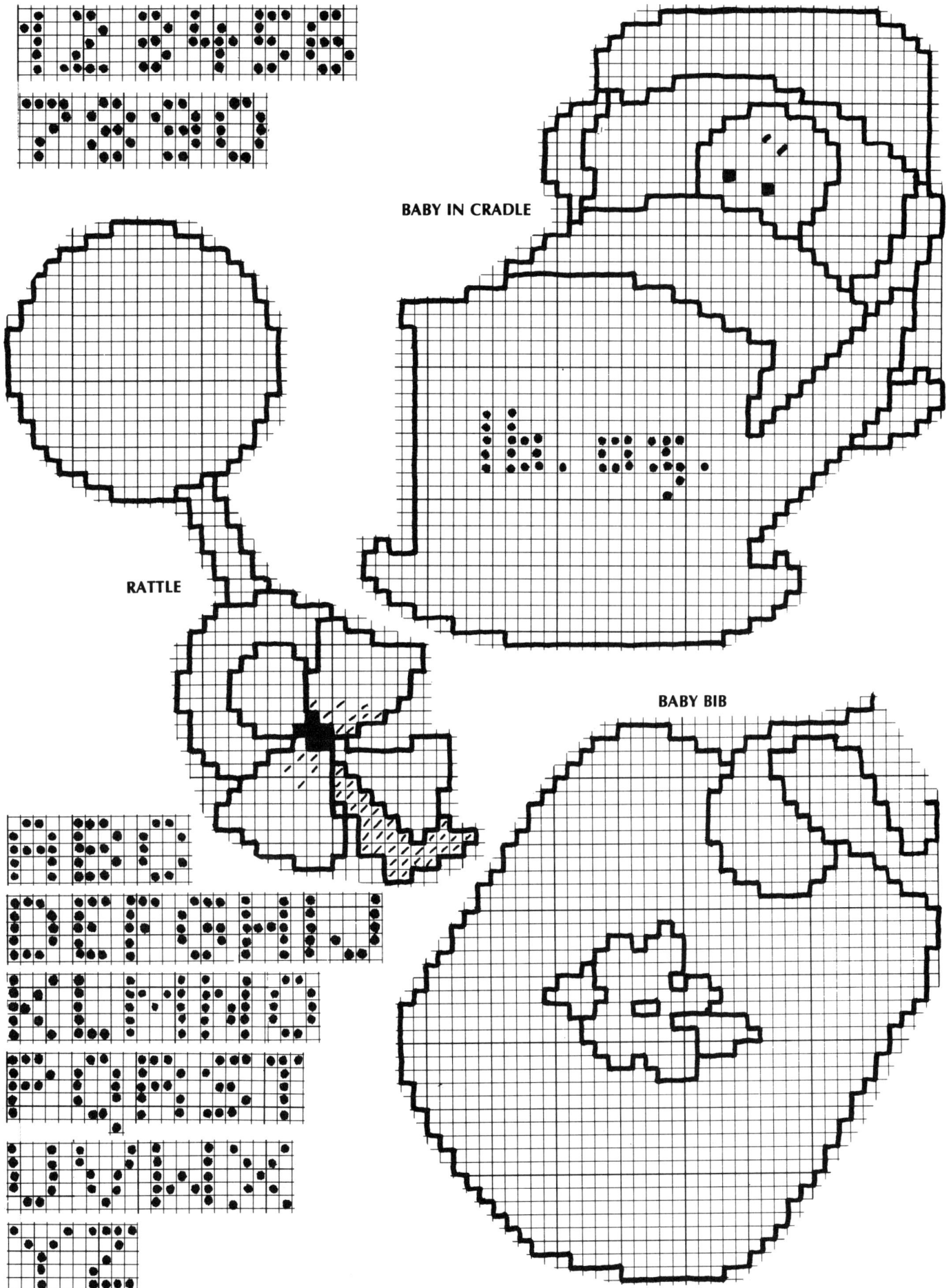

BABY IN CRADLE

RATTLE

BABY BIB

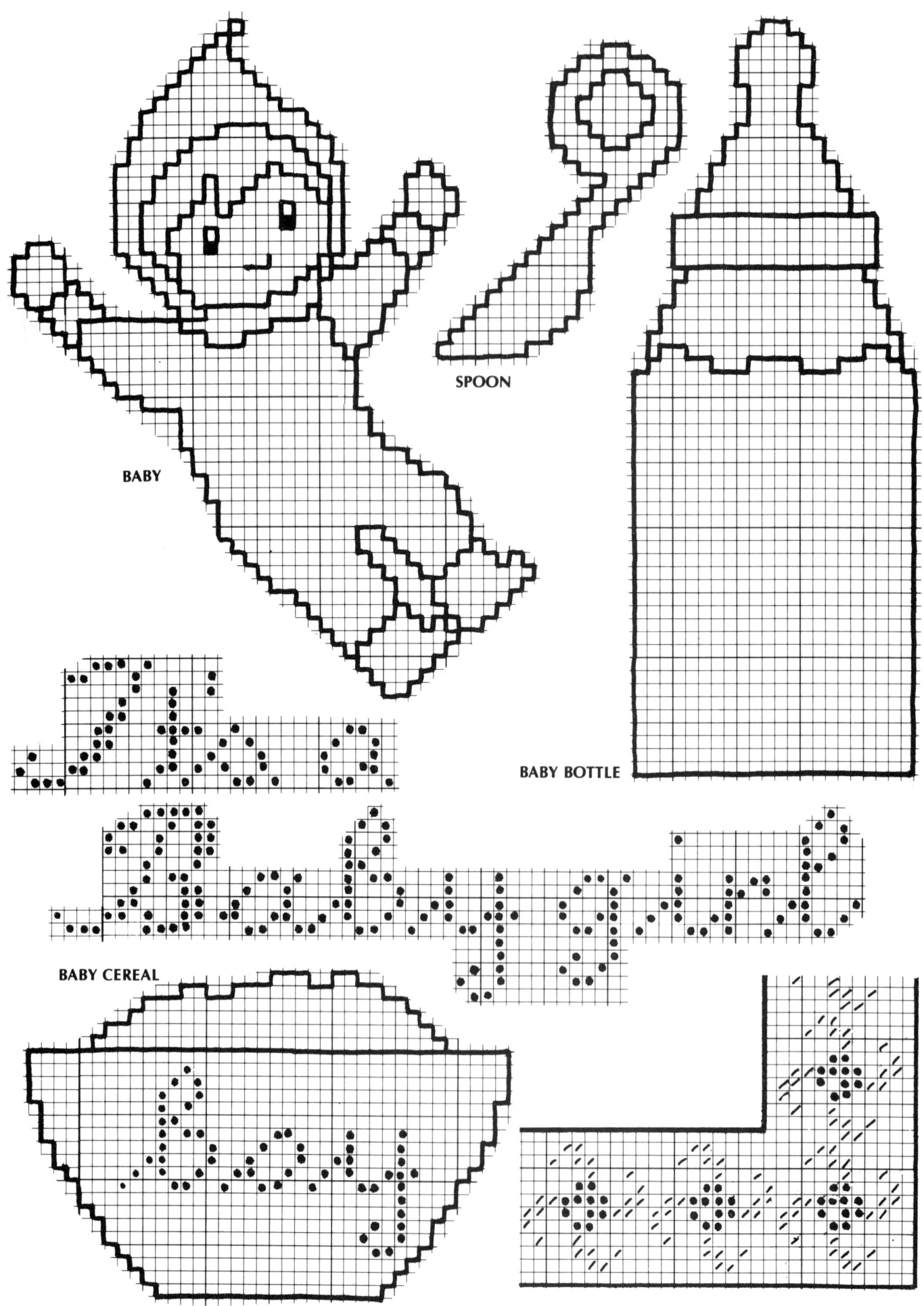

BABY

SPOON

BABY BOTTLE

BABY CEREAL

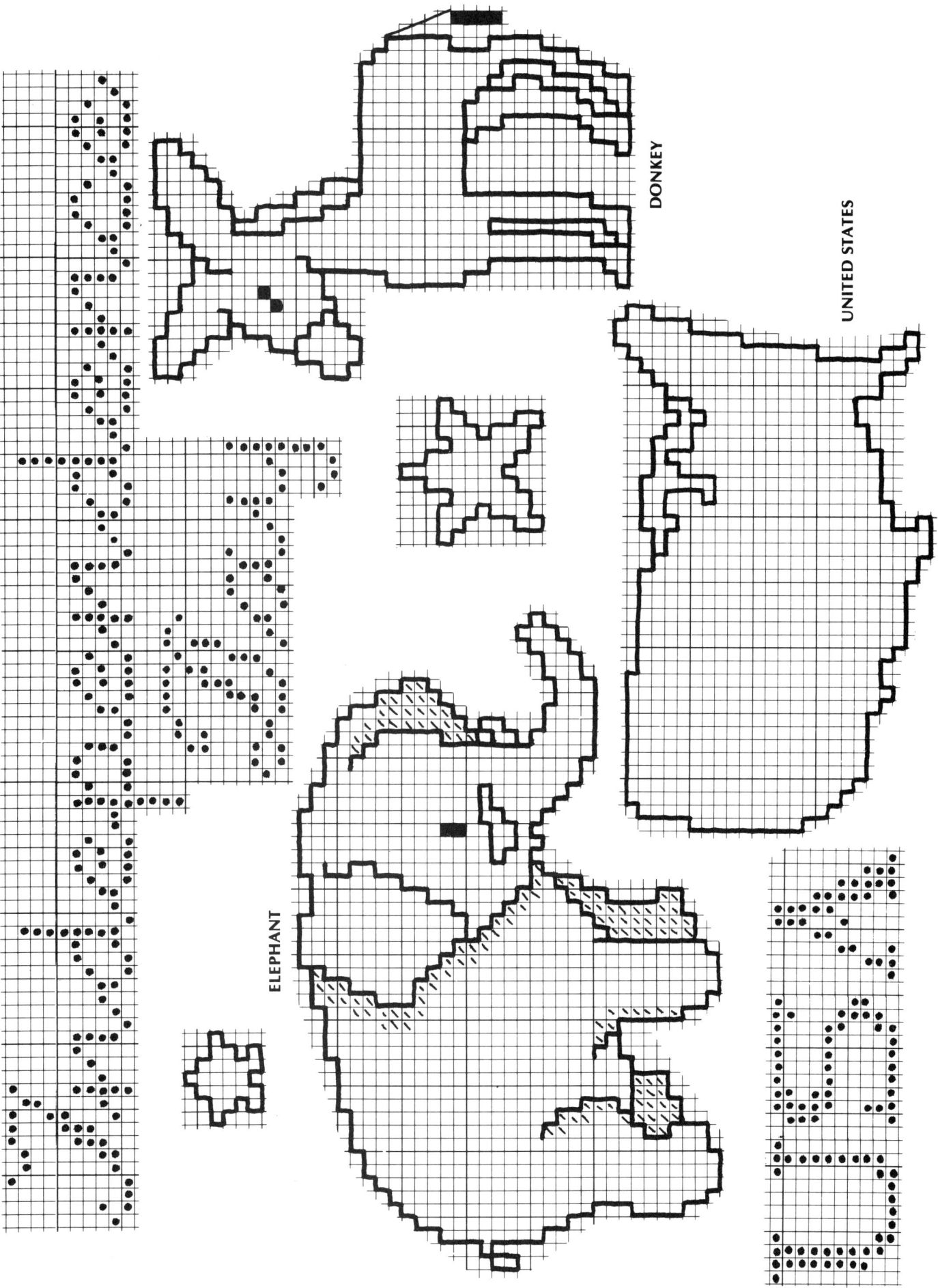

DONKEY

UNITED STATES

ELEPHANT

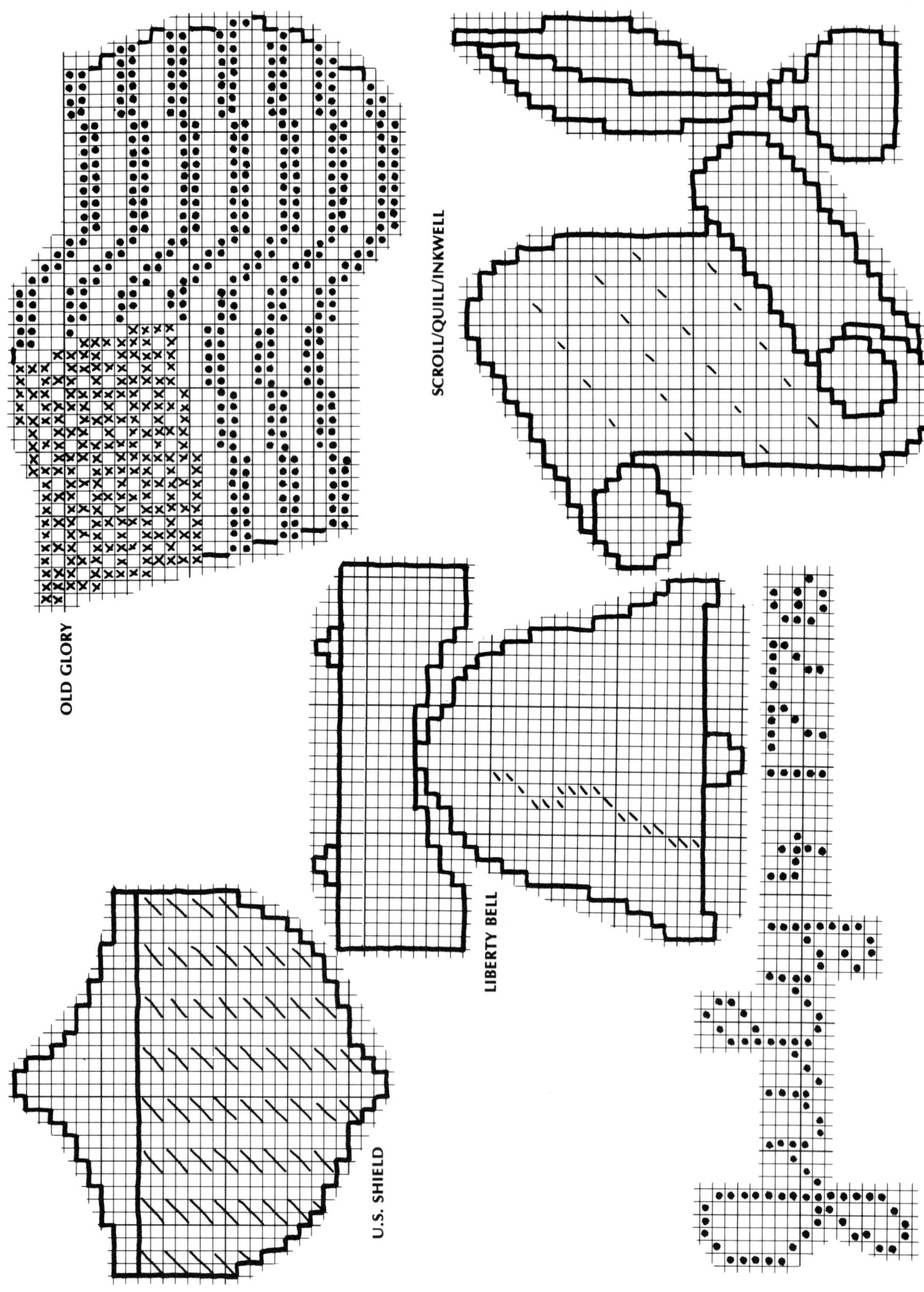

OLD GLORY

SCROLL/QUILL/INKWELL

LIBERTY BELL

U.S. SHIELD

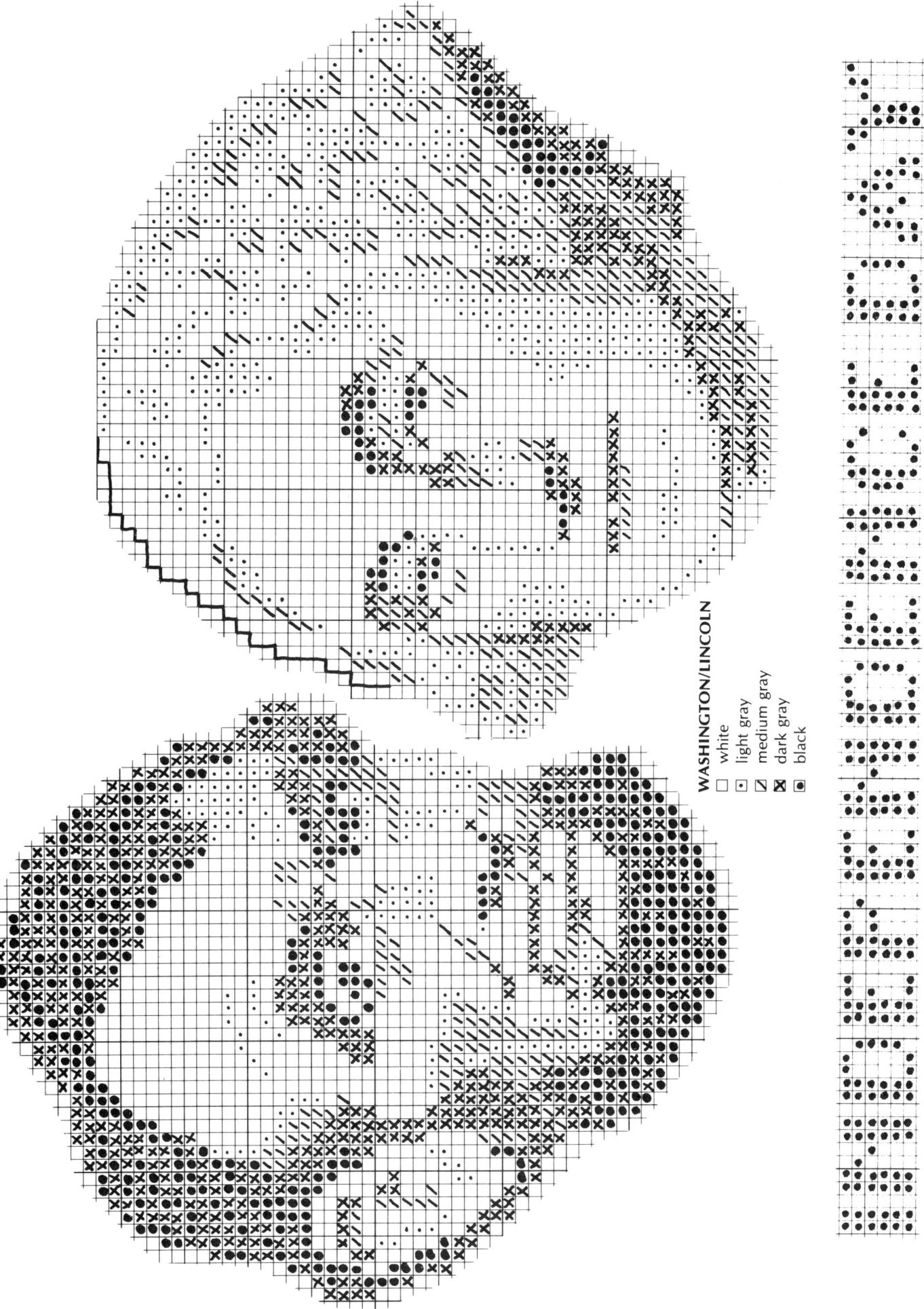

WASHINGTON/LINCOLN

☐ white
⊡ light gray
◪ medium gray
☒ dark gray
◉ black

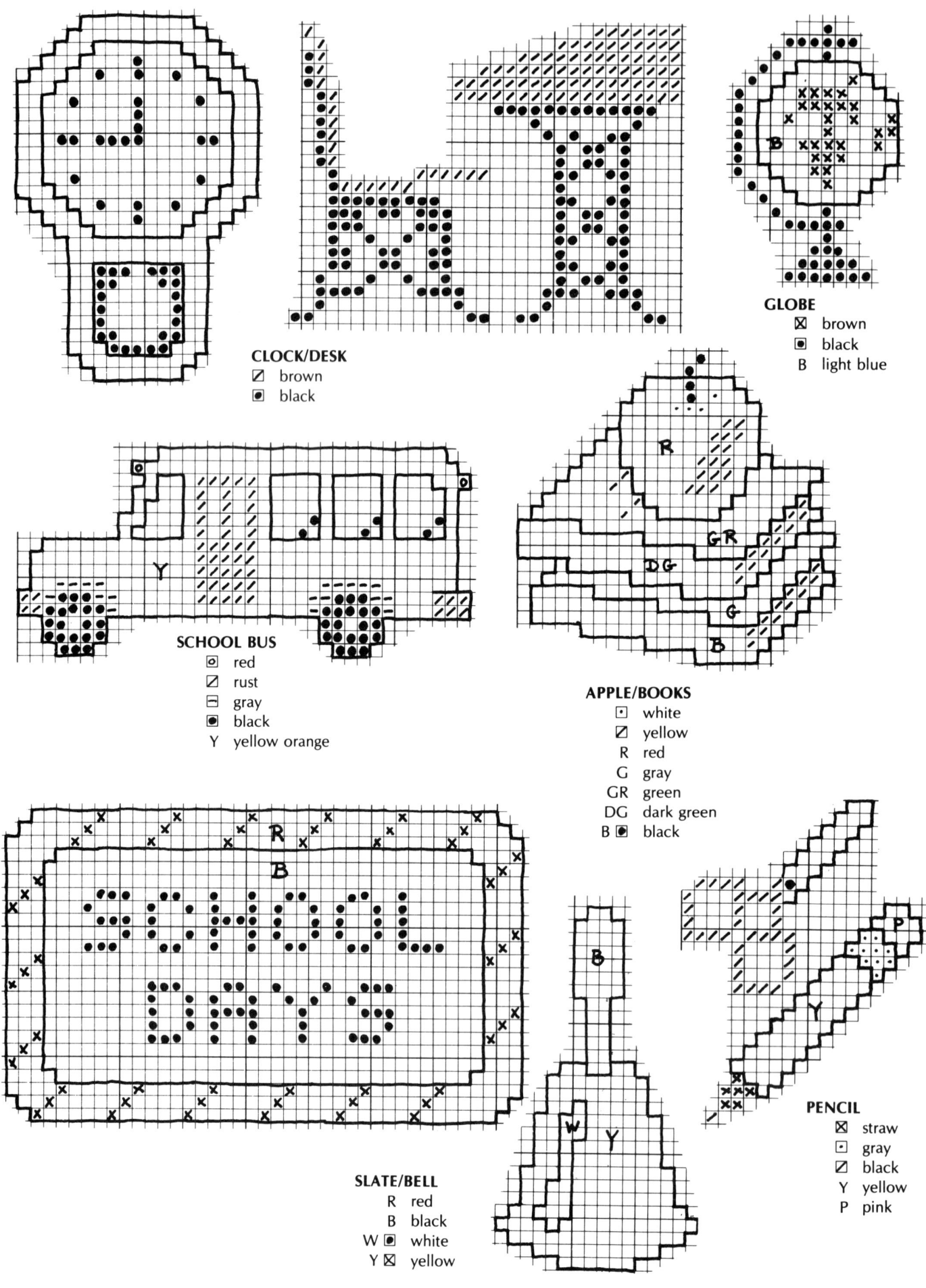

CLOCK/DESK
- ▨ brown
- ◉ black

GLOBE
- ☒ brown
- ◉ black
- B light blue

SCHOOL BUS
- ◉ red
- ▨ rust
- ⊟ gray
- ◉ black
- Y yellow orange

APPLE/BOOKS
- ⊡ white
- ▨ yellow
- R red
- G gray
- GR green
- DG dark green
- B ◉ black

SLATE/BELL
- R red
- B black
- W ◉ white
- Y ☒ yellow

PENCIL
- ☒ straw
- ⊡ gray
- ▨ black
- Y yellow
- P pink

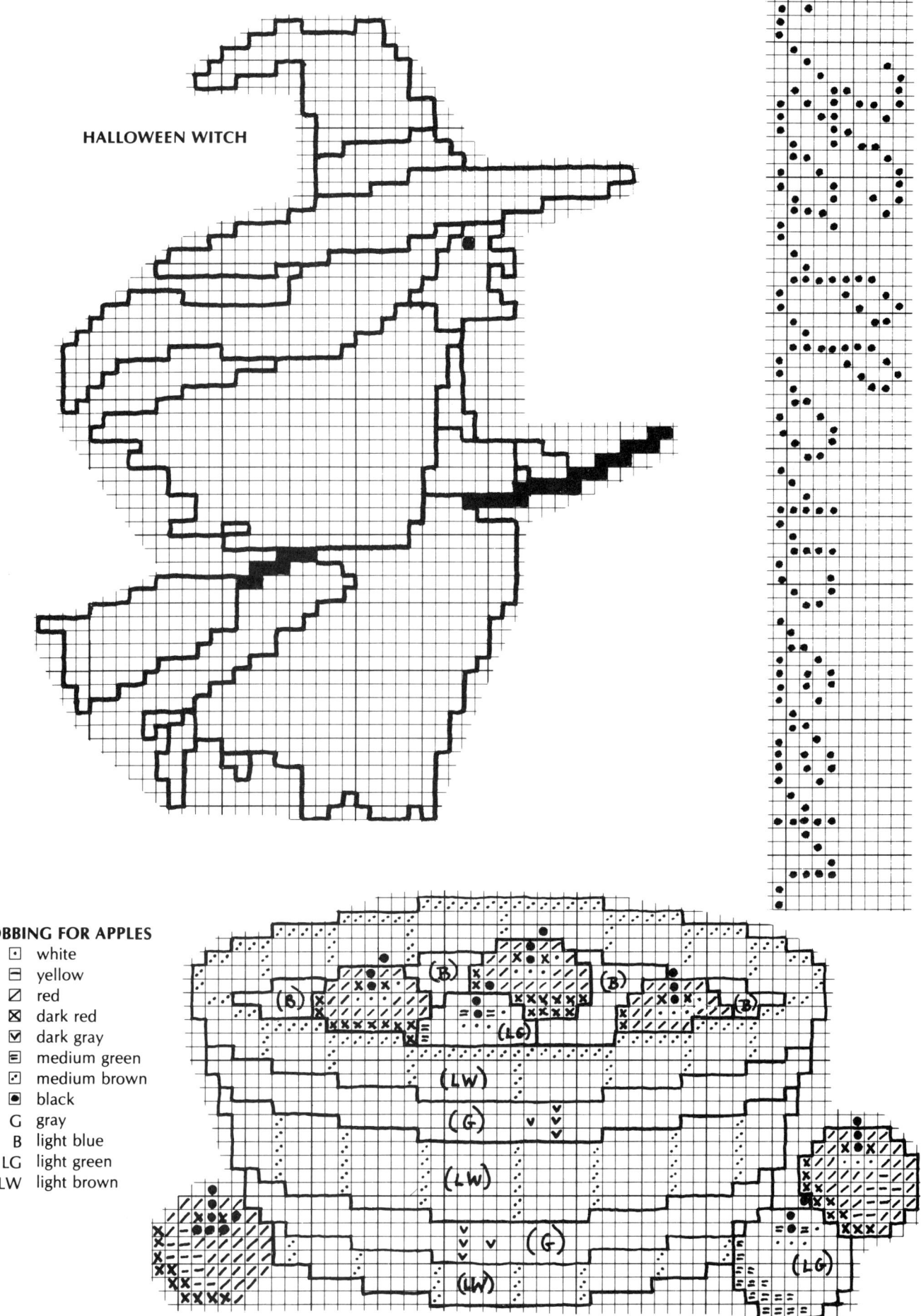

HALLOWEEN WITCH

BOBBING FOR APPLES

⊡	white
⊟	yellow
⊠	red
⊠	dark red
☑	dark gray
⊟	medium green
⊡	medium brown
●	black
G	gray
B	light blue
LG	light green
LW	light brown

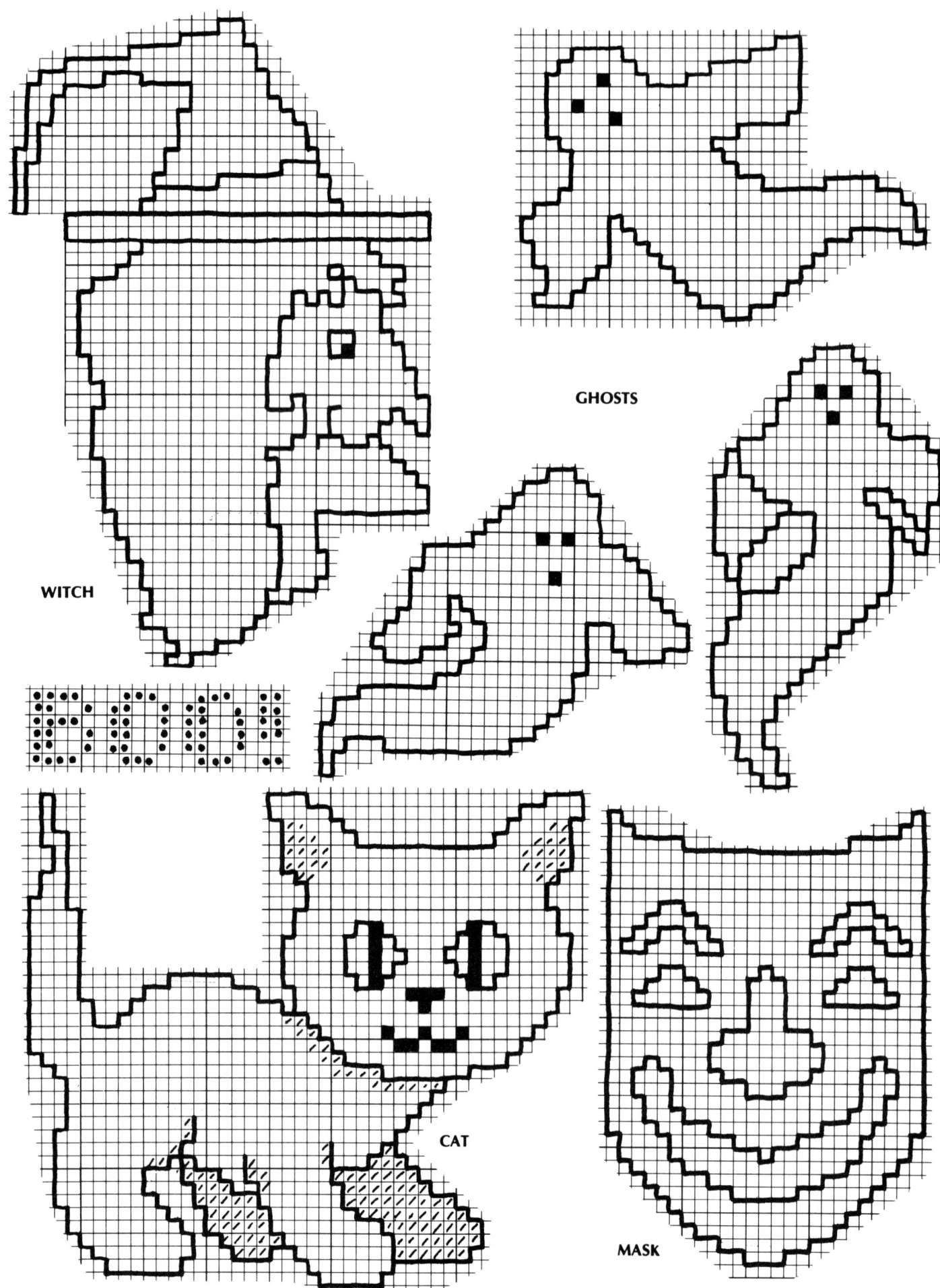

GHOSTS

WITCH

CAT

MASK

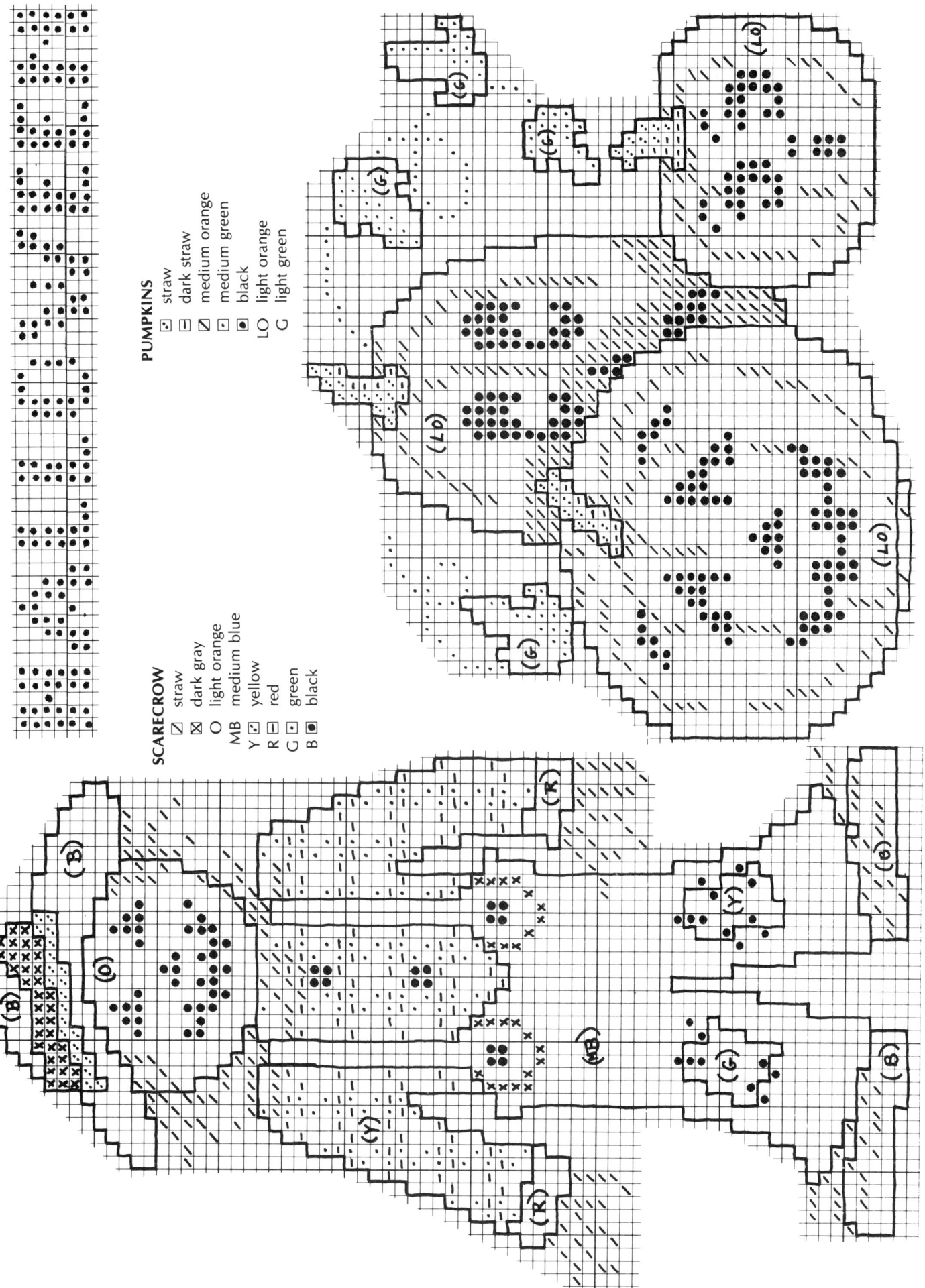

PUMPKINS

- ⊡ straw
- ⊟ dark straw
- ⧄ medium orange
- ⊡ medium green
- ⬤ black
- LO light orange
- G light green

SCARECROW

- ⧄ straw
- ⊠ dark gray
- O light orange
- MB medium blue
- Y yellow
- R red
- G green
- B black

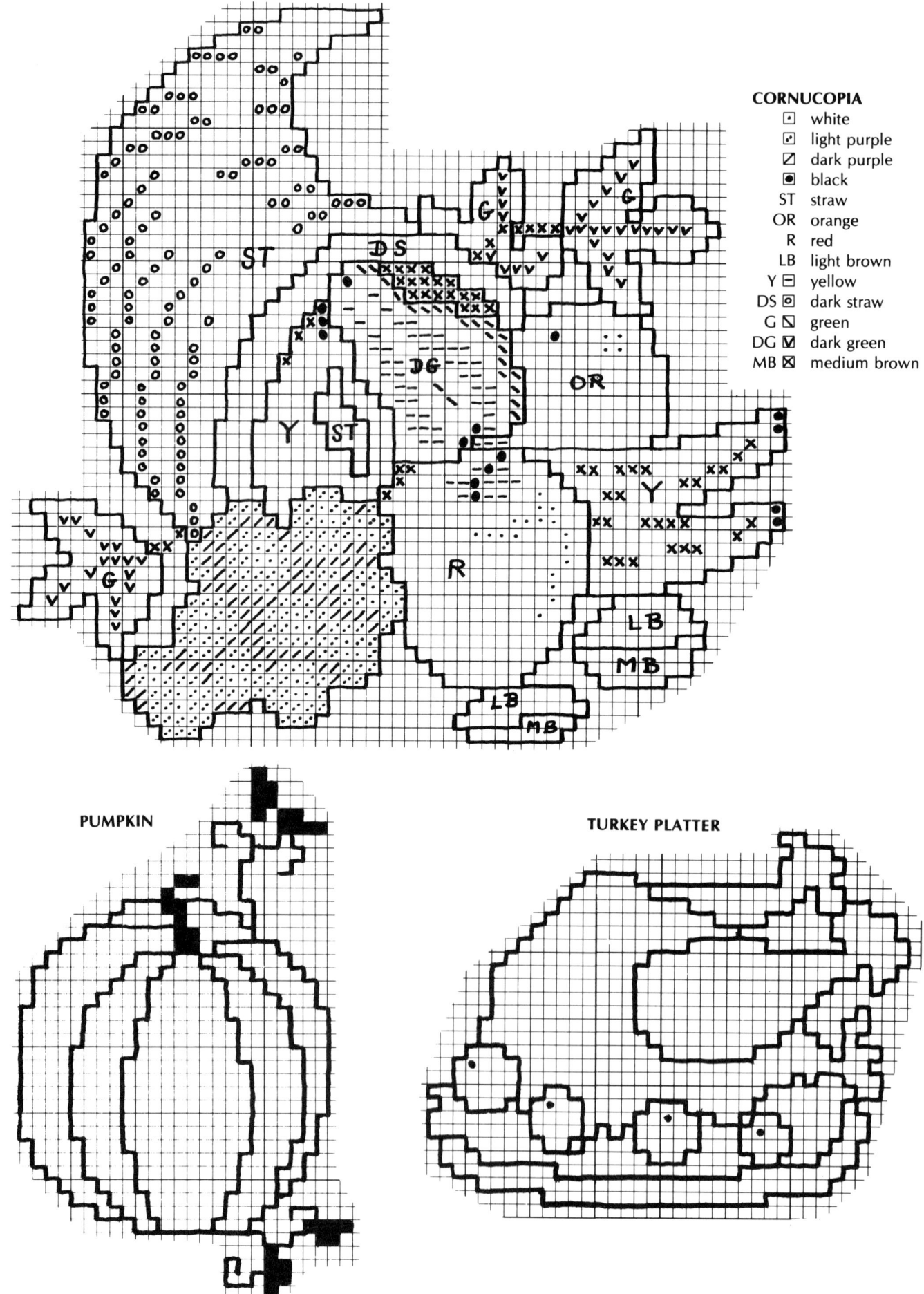

CORNUCOPIA

- ⊡ white
- ⊡ light purple
- ⊘ dark purple
- ⊙ black
- ST straw
- OR orange
- R red
- LB light brown
- Y ⊟ yellow
- DS ⊙ dark straw
- G ⊠ green
- DG ☑ dark green
- MB ⊠ medium brown

PUMPKIN

TURKEY PLATTER

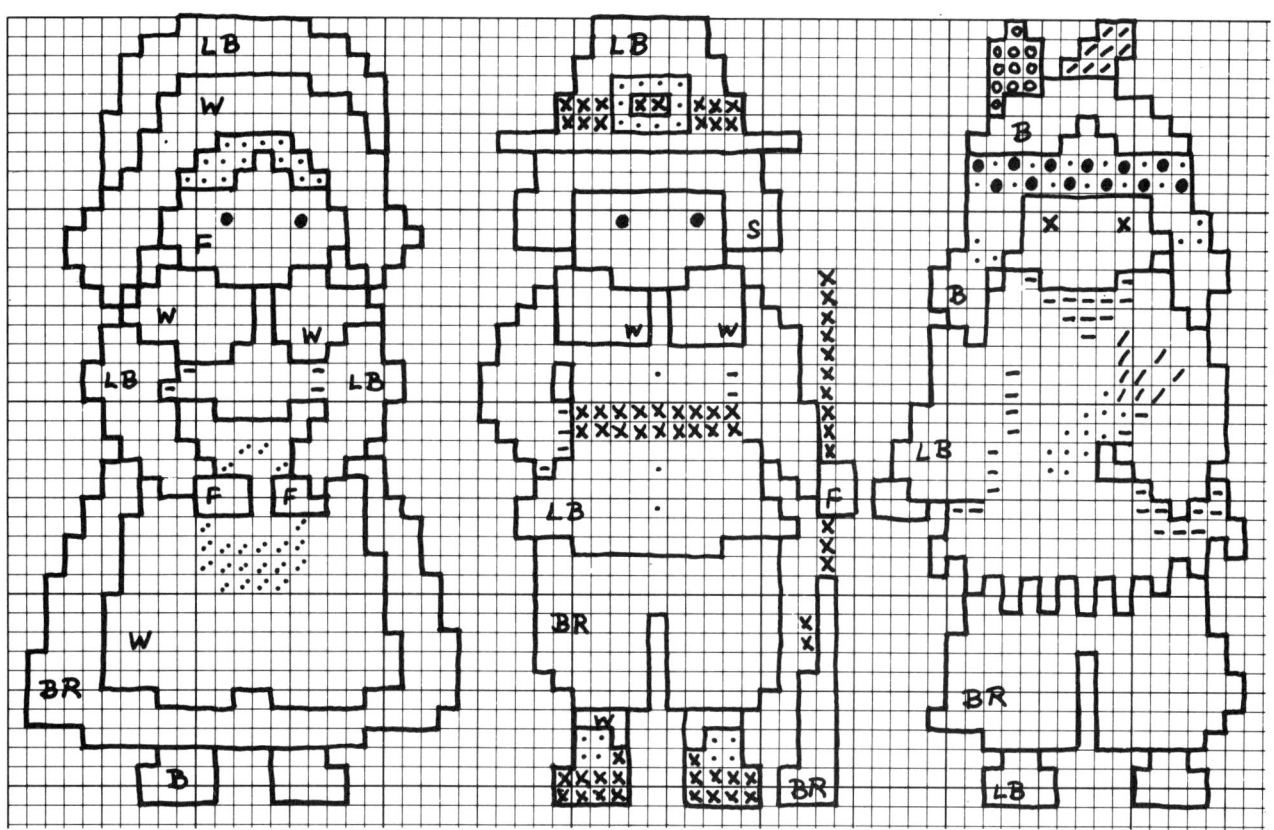

PILGRIMS/INDIAN

- ⊡ yellow
- ⊙ red
- ⊙ blue
- ⧄ green
- W white
- F flesh
- LB light brown
- S ⊡ straw
- BR ⊟ brown
- B ⊠ black

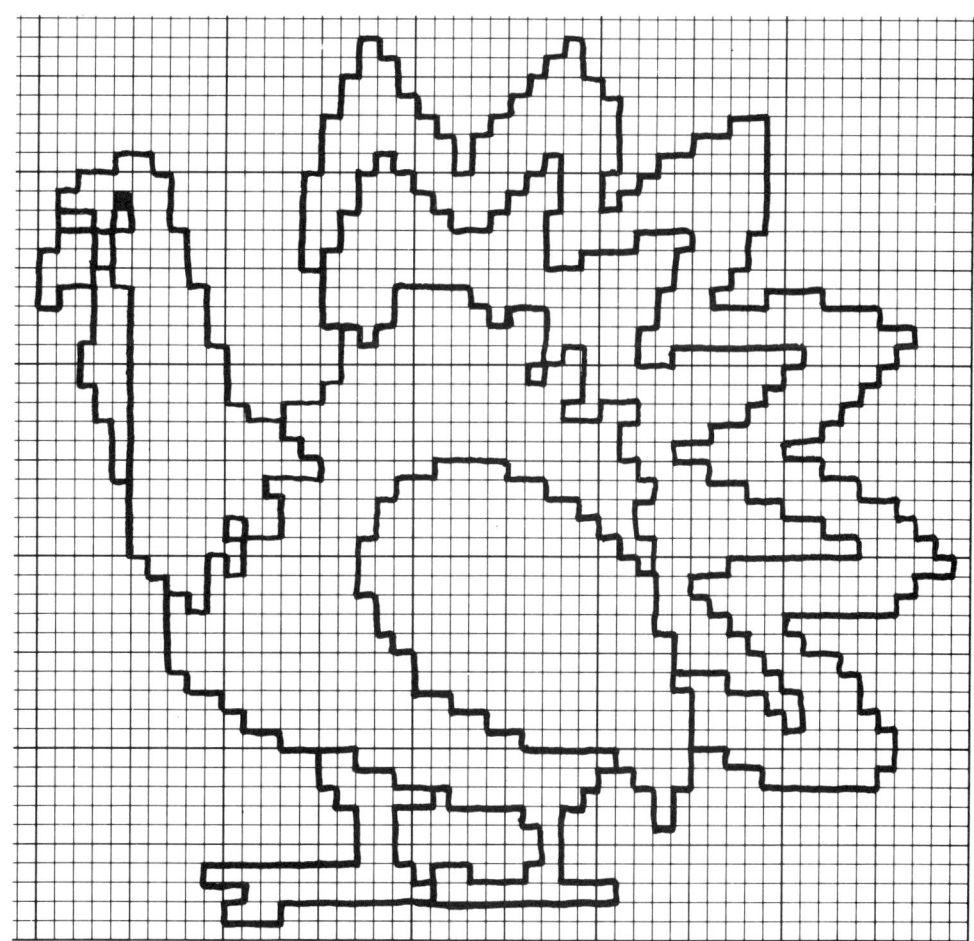

GOBBLER

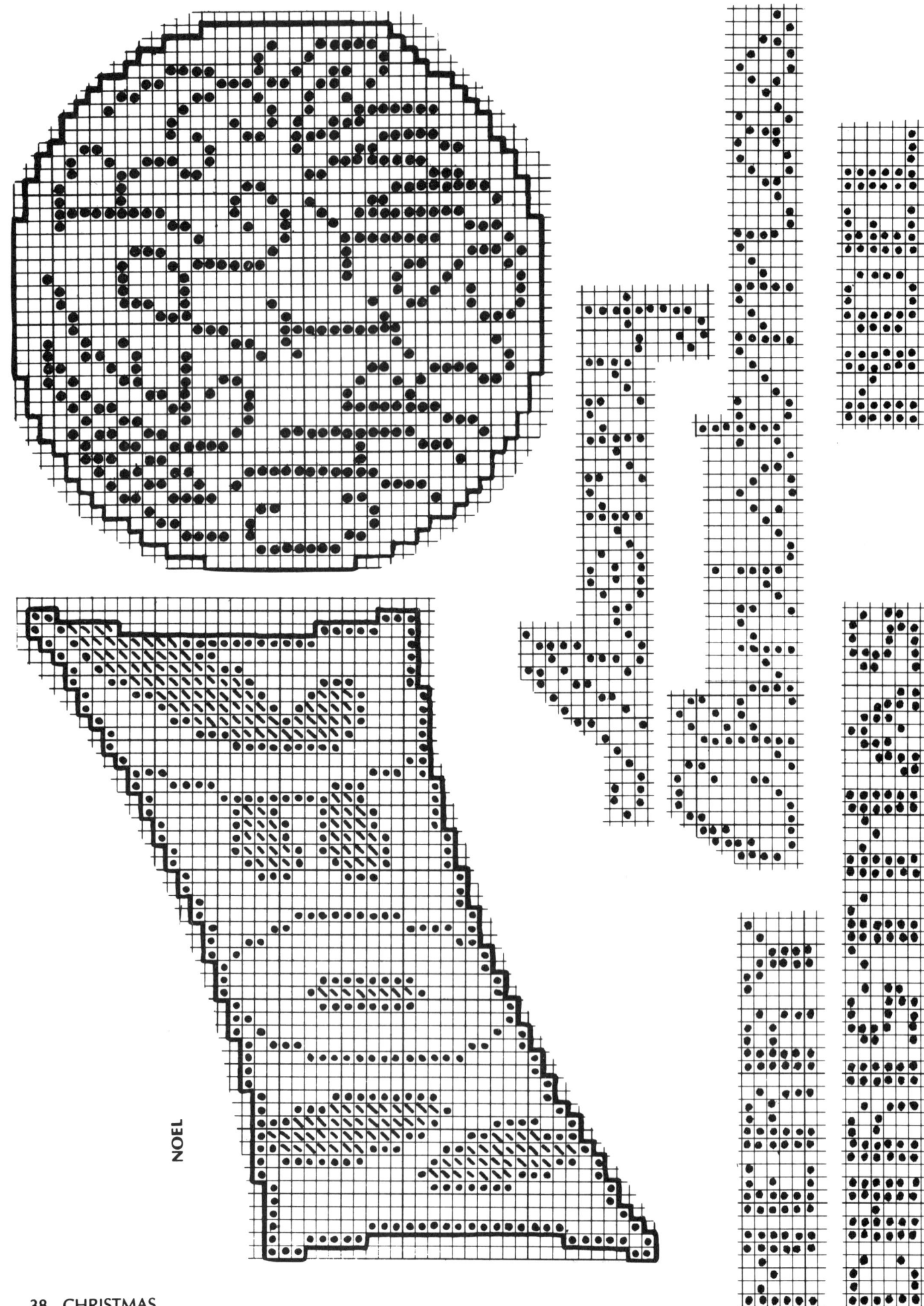

NOEL

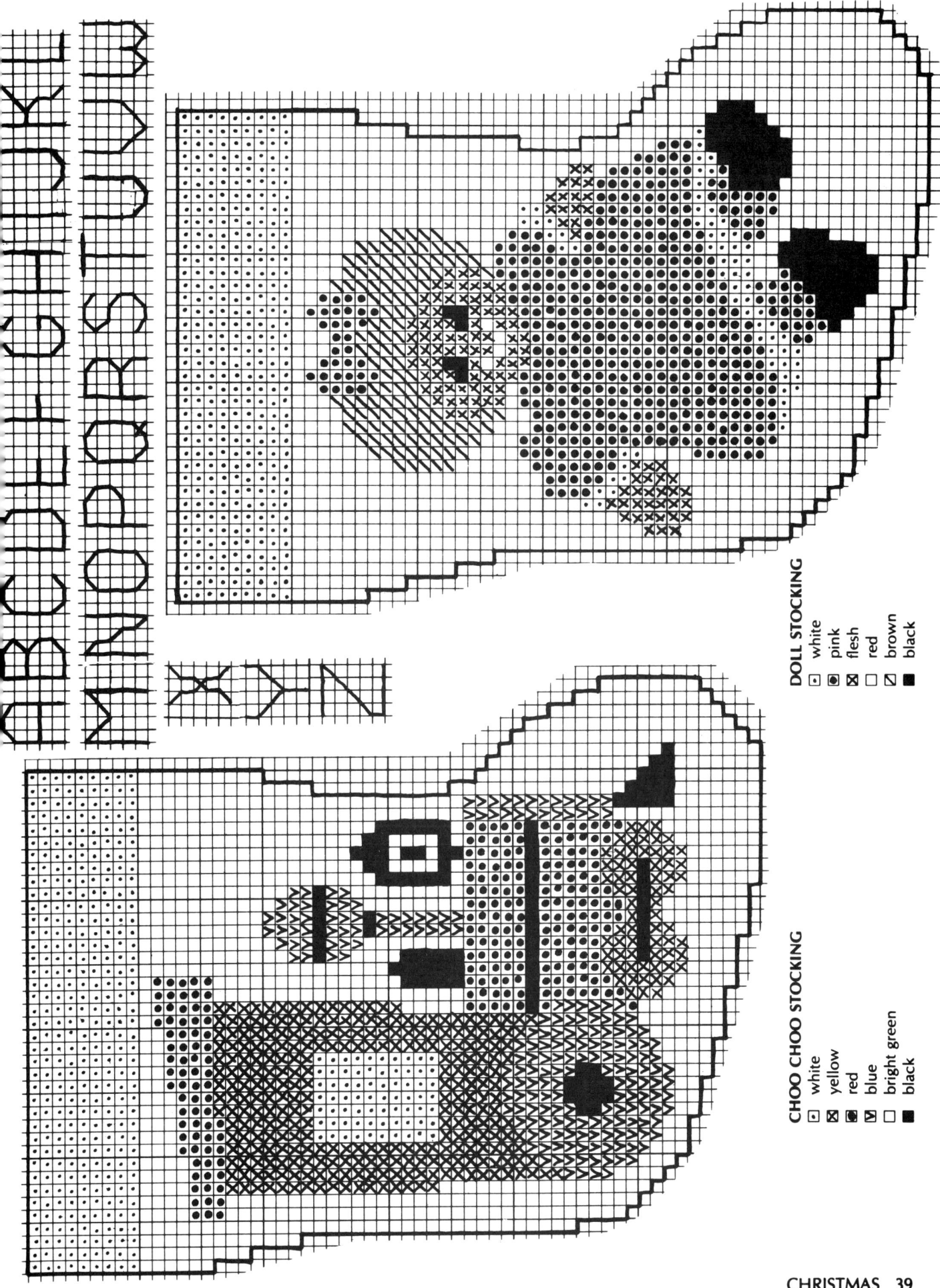

DOLL STOCKING

⊡	white
⊙	pink
⊠	flesh
☐	red
⊘	brown
■	black

CHOO CHOO STOCKING

⊡	white
⊠	yellow
⊙	red
⊻	blue
☐	bright green
■	black

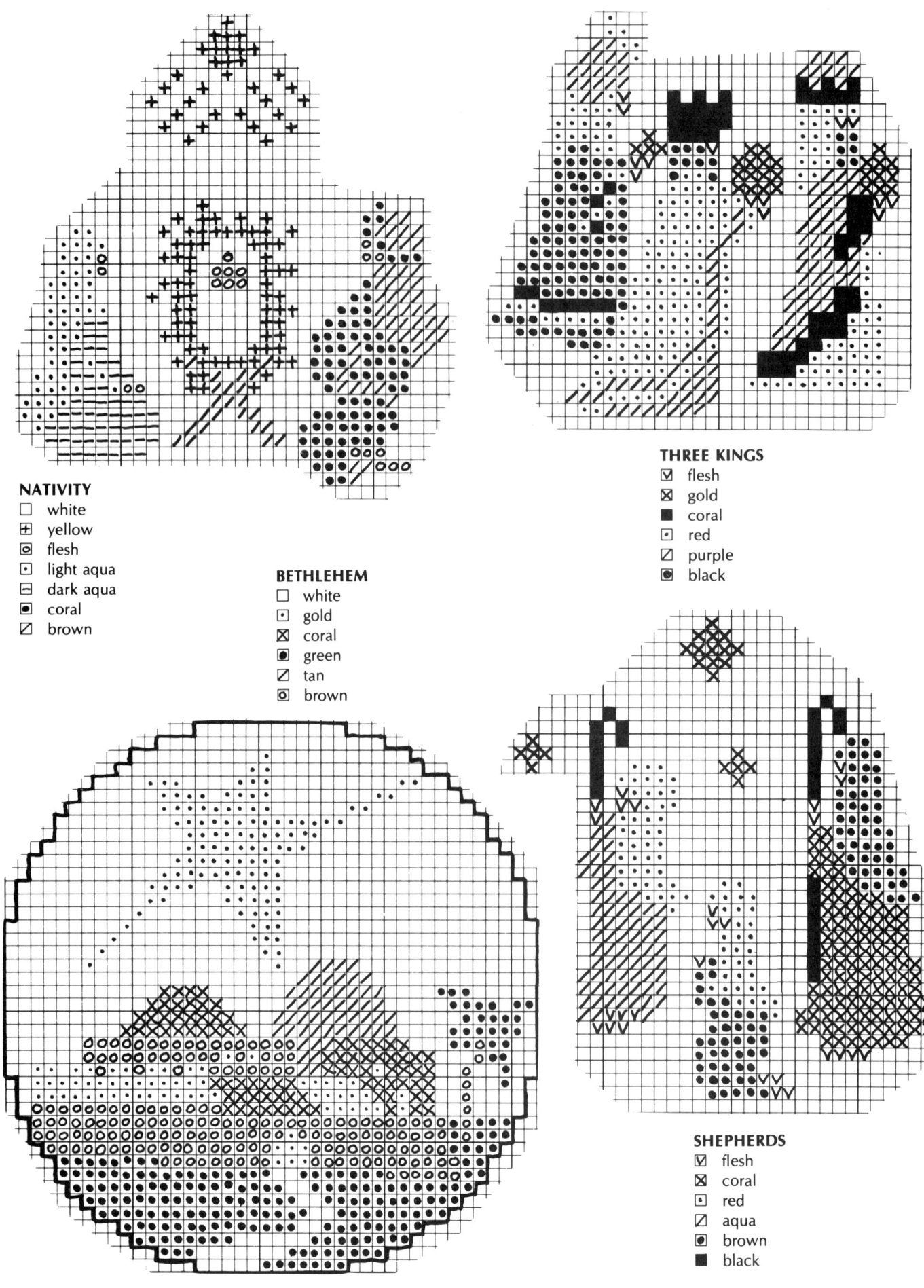

NATIVITY
☐ white
⊞ yellow
⊡ flesh
⊡ light aqua
⊟ dark aqua
⊡ coral
⊘ brown

BETHLEHEM
☐ white
⊡ gold
⊠ coral
⊚ green
⊘ tan
⊙ brown

THREE KINGS
☑ flesh
⊠ gold
■ coral
⊡ red
⊘ purple
⊚ black

SHEPHERDS
☑ flesh
⊠ coral
⊡ red
⊘ aqua
⊚ brown
■ black

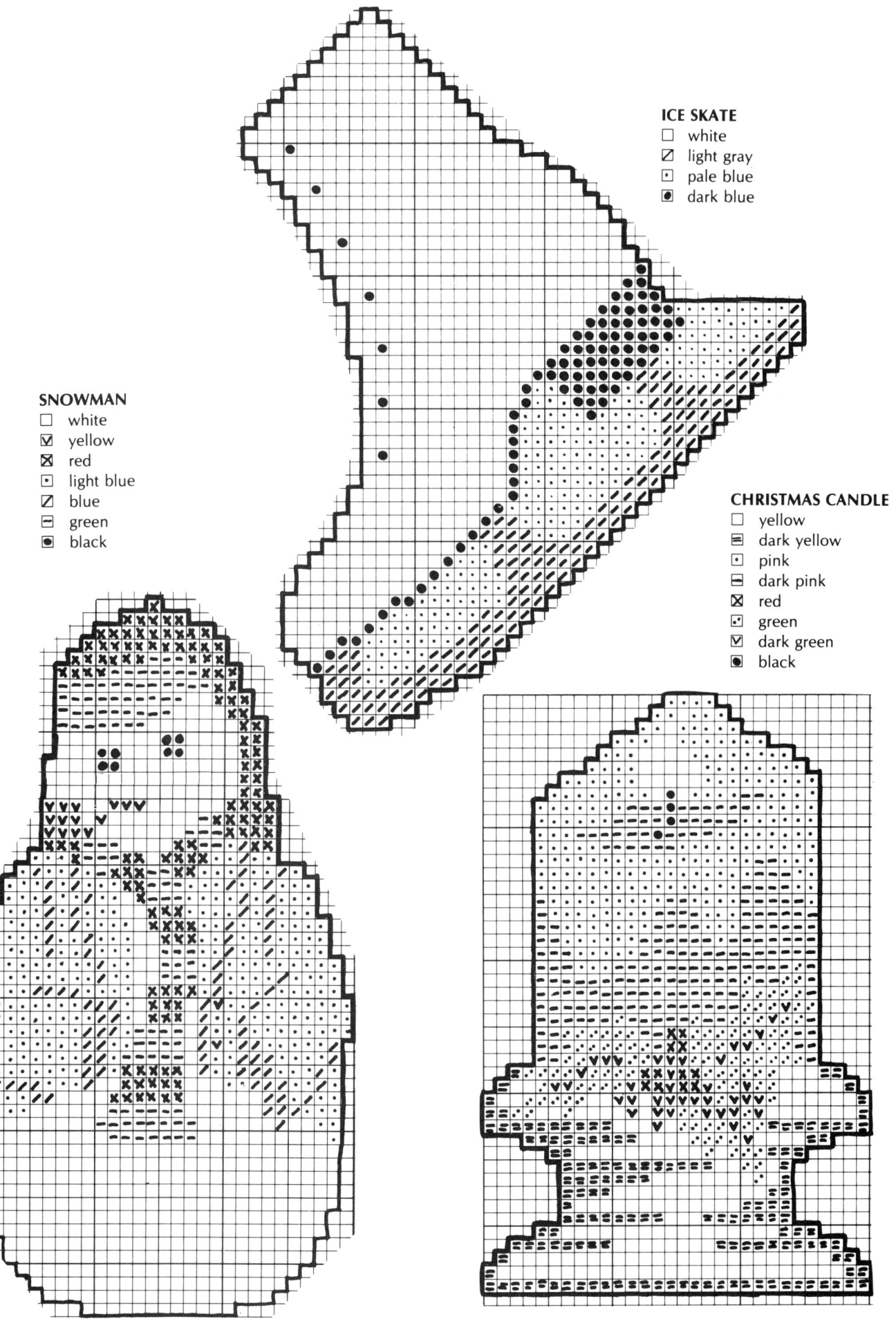

ICE SKATE
☐ white
◪ light gray
⊡ pale blue
⊙ dark blue

SNOWMAN
☐ white
☑ yellow
☒ red
⊡ light blue
◪ blue
⊟ green
⊙ black

CHRISTMAS CANDLE
☐ yellow
⊟ dark yellow
⊡ pink
⊟ dark pink
☒ red
⊡ green
☑ dark green
⊙ black

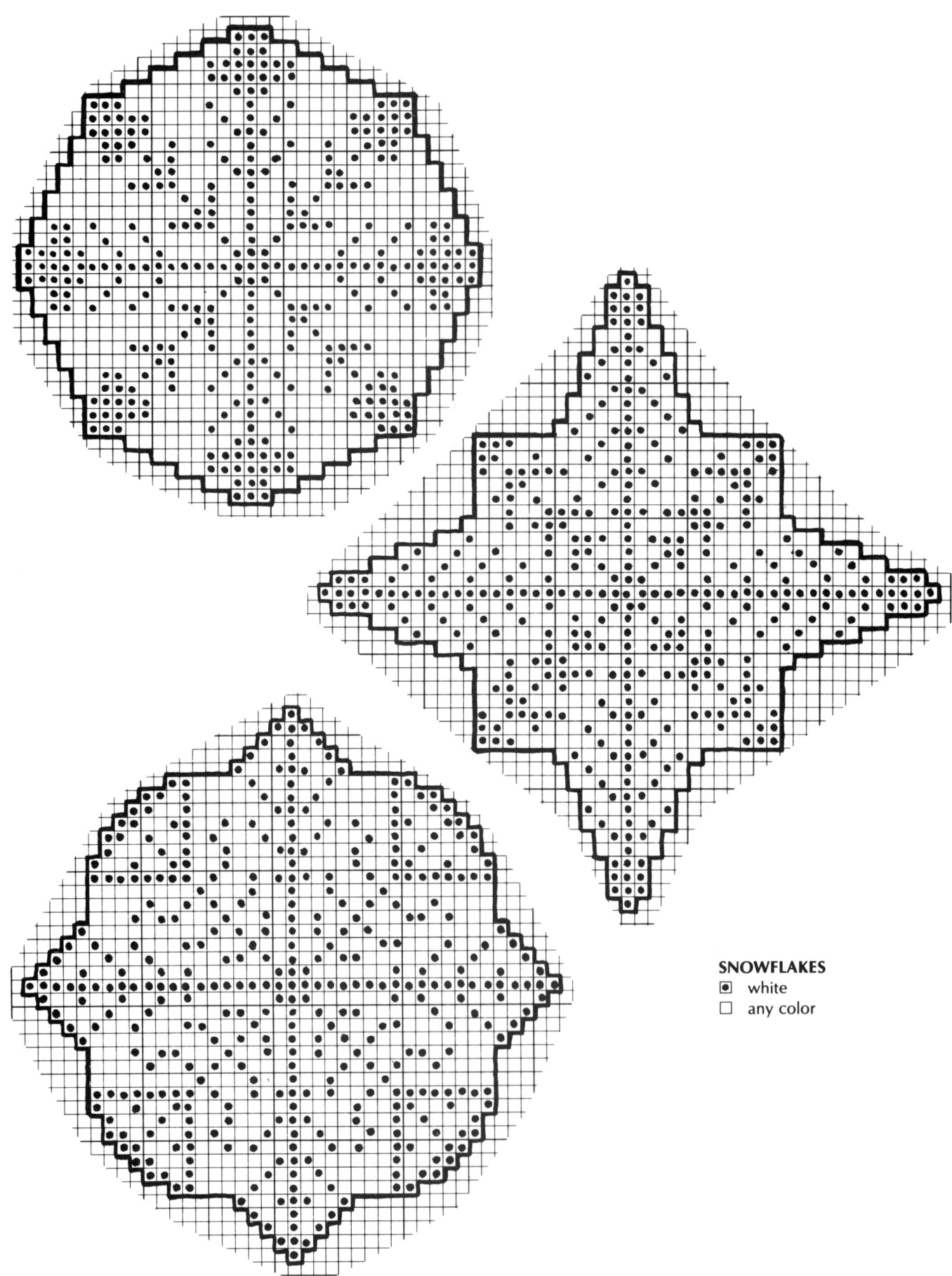

SNOWFLAKES
- ⊙ white
- ☐ any color

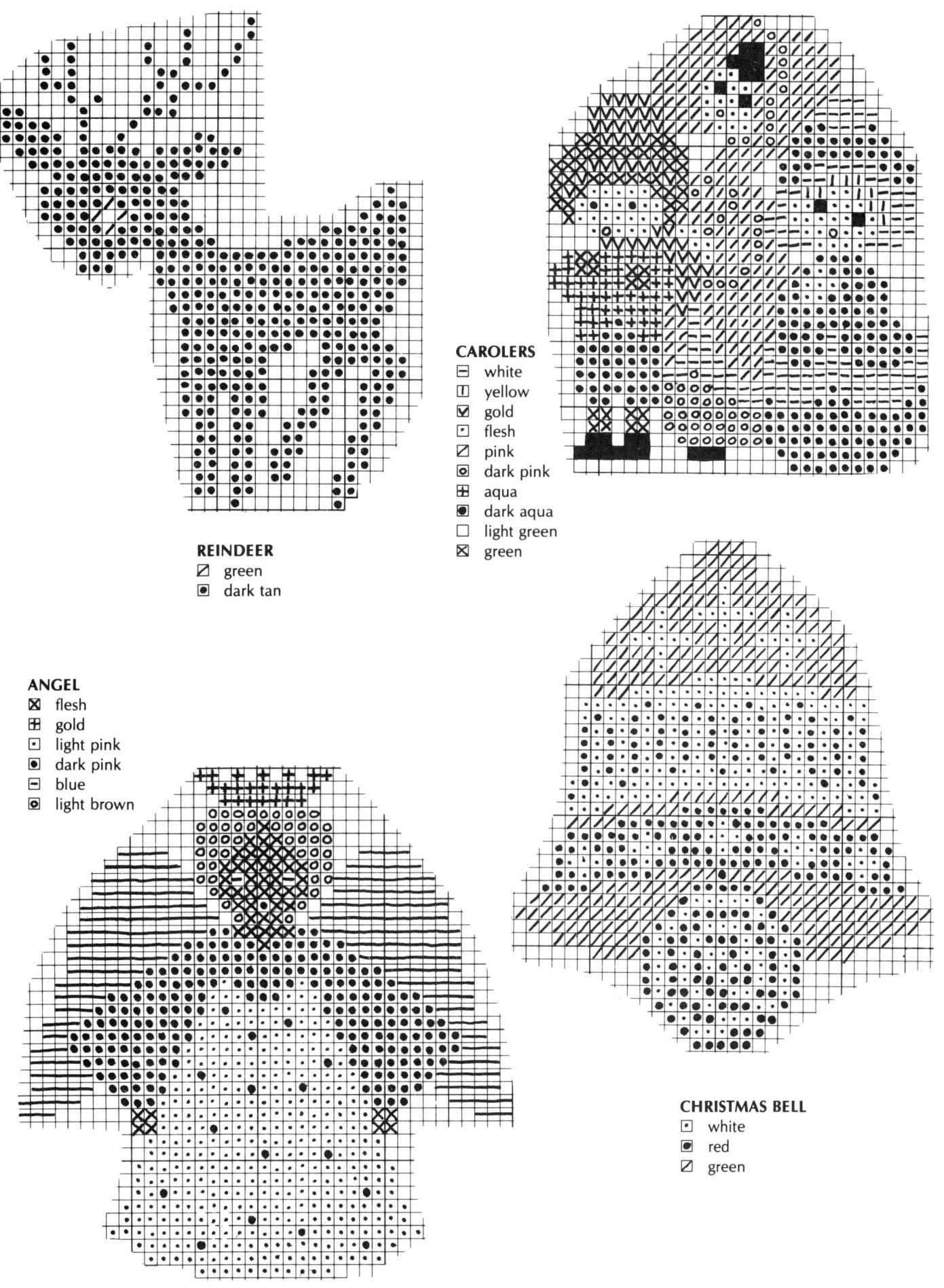

REINDEER
- ⧄ green
- ⊙ dark tan

CAROLERS
- ⊟ white
- ⊡ yellow
- ☑ gold
- ⊡ flesh
- ⧄ pink
- ⊙ dark pink
- ⊞ aqua
- ◉ dark aqua
- ☐ light green
- ☒ green

ANGEL
- ☒ flesh
- ⊞ gold
- ⊡ light pink
- ◉ dark pink
- ⊟ blue
- ◉ light brown

CHRISTMAS BELL
- ⊡ white
- ◉ red
- ⧄ green

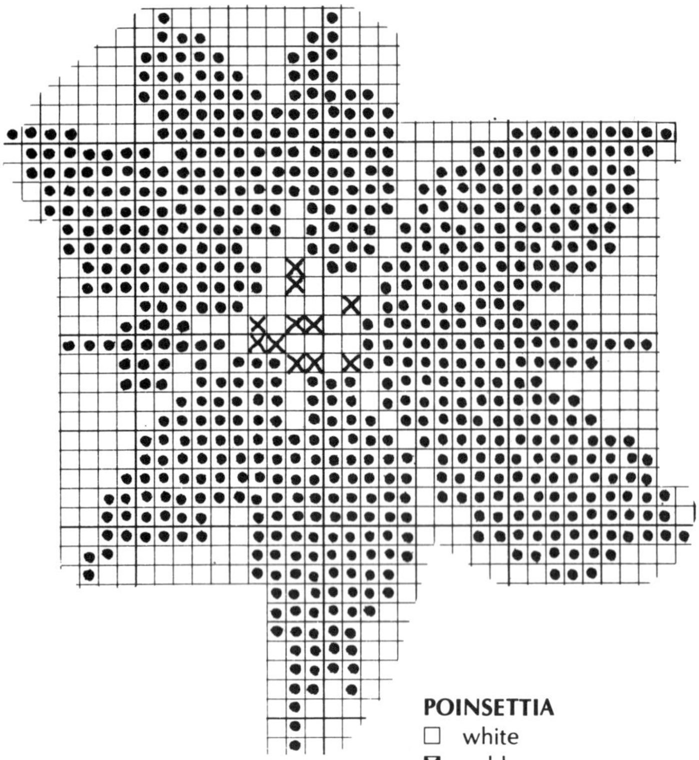

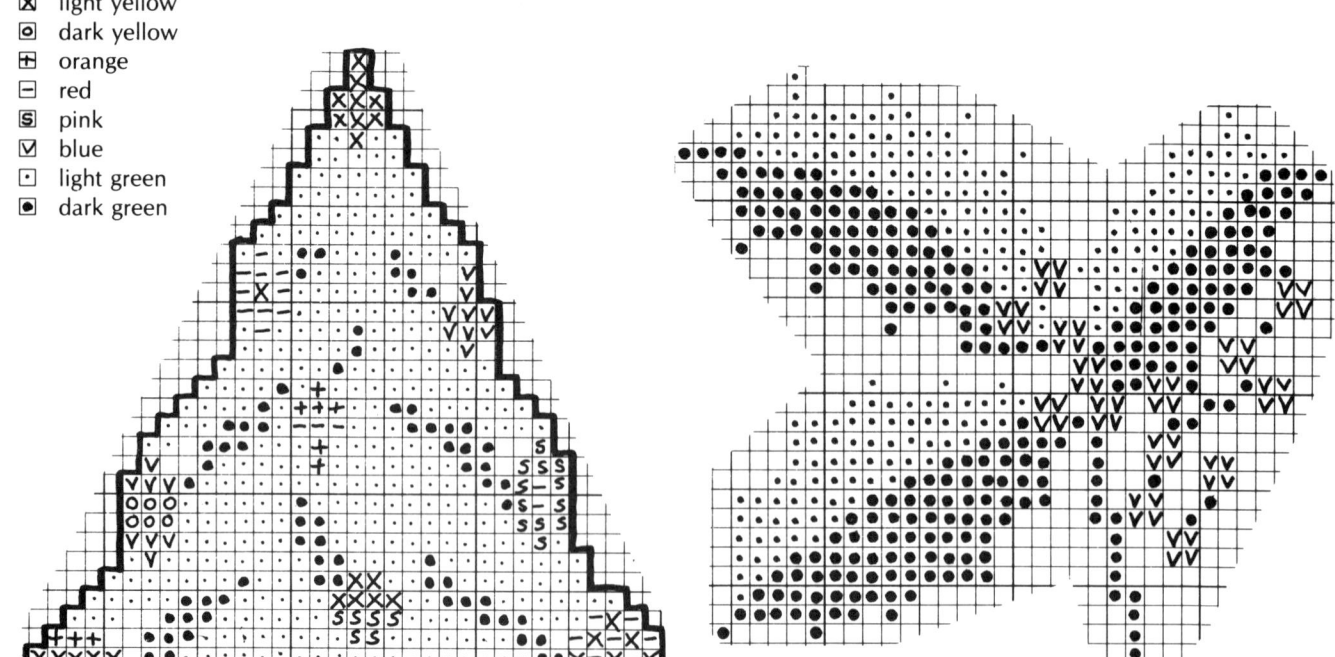

POINSETTIA
- □ white
- ☒ gold
- ⊙ red

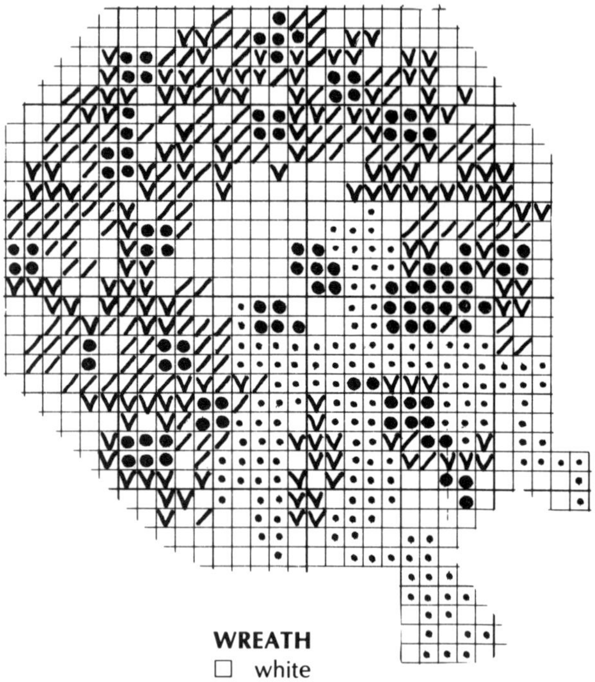

WREATH
- □ white
- ⊡ pink
- ⊙ red
- ◪ light green
- ◩ green

CHRISTMAS TREE
- □ white
- ☒ light yellow
- ⊡ dark yellow
- ⊞ orange
- ⊟ red
- ⑤ pink
- ☑ blue
- ⊡ light green
- ◉ dark green

HOLLY
- ☑ red
- ⊡ light green
- ◉ green